Man Up!
What the Bible Says About Being a Man

By
Amazon Best-Selling Author

David Jeffers

Cover design by Vivek Panwar

Author Photography by April Olin

What Men Are Saying About
Man Up: What the Bible Says About Being A Man

In *Man Up! – What the Bible Says About Being A Man,* Dave Jeffers addresses a major problem in American culture. Men have forgotten how to be men (or were never taught) for several reasons and the feminist movement is just a minor part of it.

Too many young men have had absent fathers, who reneged on their wedding vows and/or never knew how to love their wives as Christ loved the church and gave Himself for her (a prerequisite to submission, by the way).

The definition of manhood has been re-written and so men don't know what it means to be "manly" or how to properly relate to women. That has given rise to the gay rights and transgender movements (as well as #metoo) because once one is ignorant about their Creator who made us "male and female, then "anything goes."

Dave clears up the confusion using Scripture to bring clarity on many of the subjects men face daily. Every man of God will want this book as part of their discipleship.

—Cal Thomas, syndicated columnist, FOXNews contributor, author of *What Works: Common Sense Solutions for a Stronger America*

~~~~~~

In his book, *Man Up! – What the Bible Says About Being A Man,* David Jeffers has digested his own past, taken nourishment from what was beneficial to his life, and rid himself of the useless waste. If only life in the 21st Century could be so simple for most males.

We live in a time when American culture struggles to know the difference between nourishment and waste. How tragic! Yet, David offers the simple clarity so many fatherless men lack.

He points his readers to the proverbial outhouse, provides the soap and water, and finally offers a feast at a spiritual banqueting table, where every man can dine with his dignity intact.

A man who triumphantly overcame himself and lived to tell about it has mined out the Scriptures to the benefit of every man who reads this book. I commend it to your reading.

—Cary Gordon, Senior Pastor, Cornerstone World Outreach, Sioux City, Iowa

~~~~~~

This is something that few want to hear, but needs to be said. David Jeffers has dared to be a man of God, and to speak the truth - in writing. The title says it all, it's time to *Man Up.*

Share this book. Preach it. Teach it. Most importantly men - *live it and be blessed!*

- Carl Gallups, Pastor, Amazon Top-60 bestselling author, talk radio host, former Florida law enforcement officer

~~~~~~

"The harvest is plenty, but the workers are few. If only we had more men like David Jeffers, many of the things we're tearing each other apart over as Americans wouldn't even be up for debate. You'd be hard-pressed to know someone as committed to the cause of Christ as my friend, David."

—Steve Deace does a daily television show for CRTV broadcast live on Blaze TV and podcast for Westwood One. Steve is the author of "Rules for Patriots: How Conservatives Can Win Again," "A Nefarious Plot," and "Truth Bombs: Confronting the Lies Conservatives Believe (To Our Own Demise)"

~~~~~~

"There has never been a greater need for Christian men to start acting like Christian men as defined by God in the Bible. I guarantee you that if even 10% of Christian men applied the lessons in 'Man Up' in their lives, our nation would look entirely different."

Gregg Jackson, National Best-Selling Author of *Conservative Comebacks for Liberal Lies: Issue By Issue Responses To The Most Common Claims Of The Left From A to Z, We Won't Get Fooled Again: Where the Christian Right Went Wrong And How To Make America Right Again, 40 Things to Teach Your Children Before You Die: The Simple American Truths About Life, Family & Faith, 40 Rules to Help Boys Become Men: The Lost Arts of Manners, Etiquette & Behavior & 40 Rules Every Sales Pro Needs to Know: The Top Sales Techniques, Practices & Habits of Elite Sales Pros.*

Table of Contents

"Have I not commanded you? Be strong and of good courage; do not be afraid, nor be dismayed, for the Lord your God is with you wherever you go." (Joshua 1:9)

Introduction

What does it take to be a man? If you watch television or follow any media source today, a young man will become confused about his role in society. From the macho man to the menstruating man to the metrosexual man, this postmodern world has succeeded in feminizing men and ostracizing the traditional, biblical role of men.

It took me 40 years of life and one divorce to realize that the model for being a man is clearly outlined in the Holy Scriptures. After my divorce, I poured myself into the Bible to learn how God sees man and where I had made mistakes as a husband and a father.

God, as always, was faithful to show the way.

The twelve chapters in *Man Up! What the Bible Says About Being a Man,* is the culmination of a 20-year journey that resulted in over 20 years of marital bliss with my new bride and has brought me to sharing those insights. This journey helped me become the father my children deserve, and to be the servant-leader God has called me to be. It does not mean I am the perfect husband or father; far from it. But what I have learned in the past two decades is where to turn when I do fail or fall short of God's goal for my life.

I will share with you how I learned to love my wife as Christ loves the church, as we are commanded to in the New Testament.

I will share with you the mistakes I made with my children, particularly my son Eddie, whom I will introduce to you later. He grew to become a unique and special man, even my best friend.

I will share with you lessons I taught my children that helped me guide them through the difficulties of growing up in such a confused society. They still rely on those lessons.

I will share with you the lessons my Heavenly Father taught me through His Word and the Holy Spirit.

I will share with you how those lessons became a love affair for the Scriptures and serving a Glorious God.

As you read through these twelve chapters, it is my prayer that the Holy Spirit will illuminate your heart and mind and give you the desire to be God's man. I pray it will reignite your passion for the Lord Jesus Christ and rekindle the fire in your belly to be in the Word of God daily, seeking the answers to life's daily questions.

I have asked my dear brother-in-Christ, Dr. Rod D. Martin, to write the foreword. Rod has focused on the important topic of masculinity and how today's culture rejects the biblical model. Please take time to read it; it brings clarity to the subject and sets the stage for the book.

Let's begin...

Foreword

Masculinity is a virtue. That's why the culture hates it.

As to the first point, one need to look no further than the first chapter of the first book of God's own inspired Word. There He tells us:

> So God created man in his own image,
> in the image of God he created him;
> male and female he created them. (Gen. 1:27)

We learn here not only that God created us, but that God very purposefully created the two sexes: that their distinctive qualities and attributes were not accidental, or cultural, but intentional; and indeed, intended from the beginning.

It would have been far easier, or at the very least far less complicated after the fact, to create just one sex. The creation is filled with creatures which reproduce asexually. We should never assume that merely because something is familiar to us in a certain form, that therefore it can only exist in that form; and our omniscient God understood perfectly all of the problems that would ensue from creating two sexes. If God designed anything to be a certain way, when He most certainly could have done something very different, we can rightly infer that He intended what He did, along with all of its logical consequences.

And make no mistake: creating two sexes would have caused issues even in a sinless, unfallen world. So God clearly believed the benefits outweighed the cost.

It's hard for us to imagine our existence apart from our sexuality. Children are conscious of the differences between them almost immediately, with boys pulling pony tails and accusing girls of having "cooties." In no time that phase passes (well, okay, that phase never really passes), and those same boys are suddenly obsessed with those same girls, ordering every aspect of their lives so as to gain their attention and favor (something the girls are all too willing to give, albeit not necessarily to any of the specific boys who may desire it, or them).

Would great buildings, or works of art, or sports victories, or literature, or even civilization itself exist were it not for this compulsion men feel to impress women? Somehow I doubt it.

Of course, in a fallen world, in which every single soul on Earth is a wicked self-aggrandizing sinner, if saved at all then saved only by grace, this same God-ordained dichotomy produces many additional problems. From Genesis 6 to David and Bathsheba to Amnon and poor Tamar to the end of the world, we see men wrongfully acting on their sexual impulses (and women doing likewise, as Proverbs chapters 5-7 detail at length). The feminine virtues are all too often abused – by both sexes – with women usually paying the greater, or at least more obvious, price.

The culture does not hate masculinity *because* of this. However, it does use these very real problems as the core of its indictment. And who can argue? When men abuse women – whether against their will or entirely within it – who does not see their guilt, and demand change? And when the same behaviors present themselves again and again (because "there is nothing new under the sun"), isn't it "obvious" that the problem is in the design, that there's something fundamentally wrong with men and with masculinity, that the "weaker vessels" (who often bristle at being thought weaker, even as they demand special protections in light of that comparative disadvantage) have a *systemic* grievance, and that the only reasonable resolution is to abolish masculinity, today widely labeled "toxic"?

Who can argue?

Well, as followers of our Creator, *we* must. Our Creator designed this system, regardless of our wrongful acts within it. He understood we would abuse it, as we abuse absolutely everything. Nevertheless He created it, as He created us, anyway.

This tells us a number of things. The most important of them is that, absent sin, the comparative strength of men and weakness of women, the comparative sensitivity of women and insensitivity of men, the comparative boldness of men and meekness of women, the very existence of testosterone and of estrogen, *are good*. They are positive. They are symbiotic. They are aspects of a system in which the whole is greater than the sum of its parts. They are, in a word, glorious.

Someone will surely read this and claim that the foregoing paragraph suggests that all men are alike, or all women are alike, or that one sex is superior to the other, or some similar modern anti-Christian trope. So forgive me if I indulge one of the more obvious masculine attributes and, in addition to pointing out that they're grossly mistaken, I also *just don't care*. We're talking about systemic averages here, not every single individual, and not agreeing to the culture's replacement of thinking with feeling, I'm going to stick to the former.

By the way, men: your families need you to feel enough to be gentle with them, but think enough – and firmly enough – to lead: to be the one they count on when it matters. I've met precious few women who don't want a man who's a leader, and even fewer truly strong women who could respect a man who wasn't one. This point is telling: the vast majority of the population – women and children – need you to stand up and lead. Gently? Yes. Respectfully? Yes. Collaboratively where possible? Yes. But lead? *Yes.*

That leadership is frequently not about making decisions (though it often is; and many women tell us in honest moments that though they feel perfectly capable of making decisions, and good ones, they're more prone to second guessing themselves later, making it a gift at times when a trusted, loving husband or father relieves them of that emotional burden). Rather, leadership is frequently setting an example, or an agenda, or a standard. It's frequently about doing the things those for whom you're responsible are less equipped to do (which may be killing the spider, or deciding where to go to dinner, or fighting off an intruder).

No matter what form it takes, this leadership is almost always about doing those things which make it possible for those in our care to blossom (hence the word "husband"). That is a frequently self-sacrificing task. Jesus set us that example Himself, that of the servant leader, from washing His disciples' feet to dying on our Cross.

That leadership – or even the hint of it – will frequently provoke opposition. Guess what? You're a man. You were designed to take it. You may be annoyed but you're not going to cry.

So let's put this another way. Our culture – yes, even in its current form – largely expects you, should a grenade be thrown into the room, to fall upon it, giving your life to protect anyone around you, but especially any women and children. That is precisely the correct expectation, and it is exactly what you should do. The fact that such an expectation exists deserves examination.

Through all of history, mankind has worshipped power, setting it up as the highest virtue. To the mind uninfluenced by Christianity, might has always literally made right. That has certainly been most true in pagan cultures such as ancient Rome and in pre-British caste-based India, but it's also been true of modern Marxism. Indeed, in the absence of God, there is only strength, because no objective morality – or objectivity of any sort – can exist. There is only force, only the will of those able to impose their will. And in such a system, strength itself is and must be the highest virtue.

Nietzsche understood this perfectly, and put none too fine a point on it: "When one gives up the Christian faith, one pulls the right to Christian morality out from under one's feet."

It is only Christ who upends this Satanic horror. It is only our God Who demands that the strong protect and serve the weak, that respect be based on the image of God we bear – the *Imago Dei* – and not on our relative prowess or resources. It is the Holy Spirit, whether speaking through Moses or the Prophets or the Apostles, who establishes individual liberty, and dignity, and responsibility, for all. It is only Christian civilization, or those living off its inheritance, which protects the infant and the invalid, which demands the dignity of women, which even seeks to enable the disabled, all of whom were chattel or worse to the pagan. He and He alone makes a civil society possible.

It is no accident that it is those portions of the world most influenced by His teachings that are the freest, the most affirming of life, and the most civil.

God made us both male and female so that we could learn to rely upon one another, and to love one another deeply as the Persons of the Trinity loved one another long before there was a world. God made us need each other, by dividing up His own attributes in unequal parts between us, in a way we could not avoid and would actually deeply need. That inequality of attributes is in no way an inequality of dignity or worth: indeed, if men are expected to fall on that grenade, then surely we – and society – value women and children far more than we do men. That too reflects Christ, Who valued our lives above His own. Both sexes have advantages, as well as heavy burdens. That is by God's flawless design.

I said at the outset that the culture hates masculinity, precisely because it's a virtue. That too is true, as it has always been. Fallen culture always exalts sin, perverting what God has made perfect: read the Ten Commandments and count all the ways the world around you loves their opposite.

As much as Satan wishes our debasement, he far prefers our death. Our alienation, from one another and from God, goes a long way toward achieving both.

Men who will not take responsibility – who act as self-centered boys – are not better men, avoiding "toxic masculinity." They are eunuchs, useful to no one. They protect no one. They serve no one (except themselves). They can be relied upon by no one (ask their abandoned wives and children). They leave tragedy and brokenness in their wake. No one can fill the role that only they were made to fill.

Satan loves this beyond all measure. That is why demonizing masculinity is one of his greatest pleasures, and the tool of some of his most insidious and hurtful work. You see this everywhere, even in depictions of Christ Himself, Who though a rugged carpenter (!) seems always on screen to be auditioning for *Rent* or *Glee*. If Satan can destroy masculinity, and even debase and obscure the image of Christ, he causes men to be stunted in their callings, and renders all those weaker vessels undefended, prey to ideological, spiritual, and literal wolves.

It is not that evil women do not similarly harm those around them: of course they do. However, this is a book about men. In a perfect world, a world without sin, women (and children) would be able to perfectly trust and rely upon the men, who would serve those women (and children) as Christ served us all. The men would be strong, yes. They would take strong positions, with which not everyone would agree. They would do so in love, respect and kindness to those depending on them, using their strength not as an excuse for oafishness but as a shield against whatever harm may come to those for whom they're responsible.

We do not live in a sinless world, of course. Wouldn't it be nice – indeed, isn't it the duty of the Christian – if we did the most good, and the least harm, that we could?

The starting point for men is to actually *be* men. Not merely male: *men*.

The demons of our culture will shriek. Nevertheless, you – we – will live lives of greater fulfillment, marriages of greater depth and affection, with children who are better balanced and better adjusted by the combination of strong masculine and feminine inputs of both parents, and all civilization will grow *better*.

You wouldn't try to make a muffler an engine. You wouldn't try to make a painting a boat. We should be as God has designed us to be. He's perfectly clear as to what that is.

If you're not as clear, my friend Dave Jeffers can help.

Rod D. Martin, founder and CEO of The Martin Organization, is a technology entrepreneur, futurist, fund manager and author. He was a senior member of PayPal's pre-IPO startup team, serves on the Board of Governors of the Council for National Policy and the executive committee of the Florida Baptist Convention.

Chapter One - Stand Up!

"Watch, stand fast in the faith, be brave, be strong."
(1 Corinthians 16:13)

The devil is good at presenting besetting sin and temptation before men on a daily basis. If an anonymous poll of Christian men was taken and asked what the number one struggle these men deal with, I would predict it would be sexual purity.

Knowing this should not cause a sense of defeat; it should empower us. Knowledge is power and when we understand our weaknesses, then we can allow Christ's strength to be complete:

"My grace is sufficient for you, for My strength is made perfect in weakness." (2 Corinthians 12:9)

Men are by nature prideful beings. Pride caused the fall in the Garden of Eden. Additionally, complacency in our Christian walk can bring a sense of invulnerability or at least of having arrived. Somedays it never ceases to amaze me how the devil never gives up trying to trip me up. The old adage, "Experience breeds contempt," is sage advice for the Christian man:

"Therefore let him who thinks he stands take heed lest he fall."
(1 Corinthians 10:12)

How does the Christian man take heed to prevent himself from falling? Our chapter verse outlines four steps we can take.

Step 1: Watchfulness

There are few things Satan hates more than God's man. God's man loves Jesus, his wife, his children, and his church. God's man seeks to please the Lord daily and do His will.

A godly man has painted a big bullseye on his chest at which Satan takes aim. God's man must be watchful against the devil and realize he means nothing but harm to us and our families:

"Be sober, be vigilant; because your adversary the devil walks about like a roaring lion, seeking whom he may devour." (1 Peter 5:8)

The Greek word translated "sober" is *nepho*, and means not only to abstain from intoxicating drink, but also to be discreet. *Vine's Expository Dictionary of New Testament Words* explains that sober "does not in itself imply watchfulness but is used in association with it." This means if we are to be watchful, then it must include literal and figurative sobriety.

Step 2: Steadfastness

The Apostle Peter warns us the devil is our main adversary, so how are we to prevent him from tripping us up? Peter not only gives us a warning, but he also provides the remedy:

"Resist him, steadfast in the faith, knowing that the same sufferings are experienced by your brotherhood in the world." (1 Peter 5:9)

Peter is not giving us a case of "misery loves company." Peter is encouraging us to understand that this affliction is not individually unique. Knowing that our brothers-in-Christ have, are, and will struggle with the same issues we face allows us to determine to be victorious.

The good news is that our Lord Jesus Christ has already defeated Satan and we can overcome the devil's temptations.

God's man simply must resist the devil. Simple doesn't mean easy, so don't try to do this in your own power. As my pastor, Dr. Dennis Brunet teaches our men's ministry, we have to train and not try to overcome temptation. It must become a way of life.

Peter tells us to remain "steadfast in the faith." The Greek word translated "steadfast" is *stereos* and means to be "strong, firm, immovable, solid, hard, rigid." Strength and firmness do not come from our own power, but in having a firm foundation in the Lord Jesus Christ. That comes from having a vibrant relationship with Jesus through studying His word and prayer.

This is what makes a man God's man.

Step 3: Manliness

No man wants to be known as a coward. To be known as a coward is to walk in the greatest cloud of shame. Even if we were not taught to be strong men, God has wired us to be brave. This is why little boys pretend to be super heroes; they have a sense of bravery. No man wants to be considered a weakling:

"If you faint in the day of adversity, your strength is small."
(Proverbs 24:10)

Bravado and machismo are the extreme alternative to cowardice. Actually, the coward may try to cover his weaknesses with either of these two false displays of manliness.

When the Apostle Paul exhorted the Corinthian men to "be strong," he was instructing them to be strong in the Lord Jesus Christ. Jesus never acted like a tough guy (okay, clearing the temple was pretty manly). Christ displayed meekness, which only rhymes with weakness. Meekness is strength under control.

Even when Jesus took a whip to the moneychangers in the temple, His anger was righteous and included three key elements: it was focused, controlled, and caused improvement. Being a hothead (which I'm well-versed in) and "going off" is not a biblical display of manliness.

Courage is not the absence of fear; it is overcoming fear and standing strong in the Lord.

Joab, King David's army commander, was one of the strongest men portrayed in the Old Testament. The Israelite Army was facing two imposing foes, the Ammonites and the Syrians.

Joab took his best men to oppose the Syrians and left his brother Abishai with the rest of the army aligned against the Ammonites.

Whichever front came under the greatest pressure, the other was to come to the aid of the faltering force. Joab gave this exhortation to his army just before the battle:

"Be of good courage, and let us be strong for our people and for the cities of our God. And may the Lord do what is good in His sight."
(2 Samuel 10:12)

Men of God are courageous not because of our abilities or rare bravery. Men of God are strong because we believe in the Lord Jesus Christ and trust Him to bring the victory:

"The fear of man brings a snare, but whoever trusts in the Lord shall be safe." (Proverbs 29:25)

Fear is described as false evidence appearing real. Our minds fool our spirits and make us faint when we should stand strong. God's man is not in a battle of the will; he is in a spiritual battle.

Step 4: Spiritual Strength

Trying to make it through the day in my own strength won't last during my 20-mile drive to work. Someone will cut me off or otherwise upset my peaceful drive. I am setting myself up for failure by leaving the house not prepared for the day. My strength must be grounded in Jesus:

"Finally, my brethren, be strong in the Lord and in the power of His might." (Ephesians 6:10)

Men should go to work. God designed work to be a blessing to men. Work is not just a means to provide for our families.

Work fulfills us as men.

There are circumstances where men cannot work because of health issues. Also, unemployment can rob a man of making a living for his family. However, he can still work.

While a man is unemployed and actively seeking work, there is no shame in taking unemployment as a temporary solution. Nevertheless, a man can still work a few hours a day after seeking employment.

A man can determine where he wants his next job to be and volunteer to work for free for a few hours a day. Let the employer know that no task is too menial for you. Just explain to him or her that you need to work, even if it is voluntary.

No doubt your church could use your help. Let your pastor know that as a man you understand your need to work and that you'd like to help around the campus wherever there is a need.

Offer to help your neighbors or call your local volunteer services and see where you can help out. Either way, your manliness will not suffer even while you're seeking paid employment. Your spirit will be strengthened daily. Plus, your diligence will be noticed by all, especially by God:

"But you, be strong and do not let your hands be weak, for your work shall be rewarded!" (2 Chronicles 15:7)

If we are going to be men of God, then we will have to stand up and declare that we belong to the Lord Jesus Christ and that we will obey His commandments. This means being counter-culture.

When you make this declaration you have placed yourself in the midst of spiritual warfare. That means you need to awaken to this fact and prepare daily for the battle.

That means it's time to wake up!

Chapter Two - Wake Up!

"For we do not wrestle against flesh and blood, but against principalities, against powers, against the rulers of the darkness of this age, against spiritual hosts of wickedness in the heavenly places."
(Ephesians 6:12)

Many Christian men head off into the day like blind sheep heading to the slaughter. Godly men need to awaken to face the spiritual warfare.

The Apostle Paul warned the Ephesian church against being naïve when it comes to spiritual warfare. In his preparatory sentence before introducing the full armor of God, Paul gives us important insight to who our foe is.

Man is Not the Enemy

Christian men find themselves embroiled in various types of battles in our current cultural and political climate. We are losing our culture and our elected politicians are failing us.

However, those are mere symptoms of the real issue in America. God's man is battling on the wrong front. While we are to be good citizens who participate in the electoral process, Washington D.C. is not the answer. The argument can be made that it is part of the problem.

The evil and arrogance in our culture should be rejected by God's man. He must protect his family and home from the filth that masquerades itself as entertainment. Nevertheless, our culture reflects our heartbeat and the impression is one of a sick and wicked heart.

Looking through a biblical lens, we see the devil has done a bang-up job on America.

In his chilling book, *A Nefarious Plot,* my good buddy Steve Deace writes about a demon general named Nefarious whose job is to take down America. Speaking as Nefarious, Deace writes:

> To figure you out I had to turn your greatest strength as a people, and what it was that made you such a pest to those of us down here, against you. Once I did that, you graciously started playing right into our hands.
>
> In fact, the plan worked even better than I had hoped it might.

What was the plan? Well, you need to read the book because you'll be amazed at how clearly Steve defines America's downfall. However, I will tell you that the darkness of which Steve writes is real.

How did this darkness come to America? Very simple; turn the lights off in your house at night. What happened? Did it become dark? Darkness is the absence of light. God created light and saw that it was good:

"In the beginning God created the heavens and the earth. The earth was without form, and void; and darkness was on the face of the deep. And the Spirit of God was hovering over the face of the waters. Then God said, 'Let there be light'; and there was light." (Genesis 1:3)

That explains the physical darkness, but what God's man needs to understand is the battle between spiritual light and darkness. We know that Jesus has called us to be salt and light, but do we understand why our Lord calls us to the light? Where do we find spiritual light to defeat the darkness? Jesus told us how:

"The lamp of the body is the eye. Therefore, when your eye is good, your whole body also is full of light. But when your eye is bad, your body also is full of darkness. Therefore take heed that the light which is in you is not darkness. If then your whole body is full of light, having no part dark, the whole body will be full of light, as when the bright shining of a lamp gives you light." (Luke 11:34-36)

Jesus is teaching us that our eyes are the portals through which light enters our bodies. Does Jesus mean that our bodies are literally full of physical light and without it, they are full of darkness?

Our Lord is teaching us that we receive spiritual light through our eyes, and without this light we suffer spiritual blindness. Knowing this gives greater meaning to a familiar passage from the Psalms:

"Your word is a lamp to my feet and a light to my path."
(Psalm 119:105)

Our spiritual light comes from seeking God's Word daily. We will look closer in Chapter 5 at the need to study our bibles but go ahead and get a head start if you've neglected it.

The Real Enemy

The Apostle Paul wrote that we battle with an unseen enemy. I remember the old science fiction movie "The Invisible Man," played by Claude Rains. I always thought that it would be so cool to have that power. That way I could knock out my enemies without them knowing it was coming or that I was the culprit.

What was a childhood fantasy has become a lifelong lesson, of which I am the one being knocked out. The difference is that I should know that it is coming and from where and whom.

However, I allow myself to be distracted by what I believe to be the real battles, when they're actually just cultural skirmishes in which I should not invest all my time. I need to keep my focus on the real enemy:

"You therefore must endure hardship as a good soldier of Jesus Christ. No one engaged in warfare entangles himself with the affairs of this life, that he may please him who enlisted him as a soldier."
(2 Timothy 2:3-4)

God has given me a platform in the field of politics of which I should be a good steward. I am learning that an important part of that stewardship is the amount of time I invest in politics.

Furthermore, I must guard my heart so I do not become bitter or cocky when fighting the cultural battles. If I am not careful, I can use the truth as a sledgehammer. Again, Jesus is my example of how to approach all things in life:

"And the Word became flesh and dwelt among us, and we beheld His glory, the glory as of the only begotten of the Father, full of grace and truth." (John 1:14)

"...full of grace and truth." There is the balance I must strike. To quote my pastor, "Too much truth is a sledgehammer; too much grace is sugar water." The balance for any issue in life can be found if I seek Jesus' heart through His word and prayer. The Holy Spirit will guide my actions if I allow Him.

Not only do I find the needed balance of how to deal with the issues in life, but I also learn to recognize and resist wickedness. Our true enemy is sin and the father of lies, Satan. Of course, we do not face Satan directly, but we do have to face many who do his work. They are constantly working to oppose God's man:

"The wicked plots against the just, and gnashes at him with his teeth."
(Psalm 37:12)

The Veritas Project, created by James O'Keefe, has unveiled many of the wicked plots by those doing Satan's work. O'Keefe has exposed Planned Parenthood, CNN, and the New York Times and their desire to push their godless agendas.

The Solution

While it is right to be outraged by such deceit, it is not enough. We must stand against attacks against the unborn, and the lies and deceit from the media and academia, just to name a few.

We take our stand by standing on the Truth.

It is only the Truth found in God's Word that we can actually *wrestle against the rulers of the darkness of this age.* The Truth will help you recognize wickedness. The Truth will help you resist *against spiritual hosts of wickedness.*

This means men of God are going to have to rise up early in the morning and get into the Word...

Chapter Three - Rise Up!

"I rise before the dawning of the morning, and cry for help;
I hope in Your word."
(Psalm 119:147)

How do you spend your morning? Your alarm goes off, you stumble into the bathroom to prepare for the day; making sure the coffee pot is brewing your life-giving fluids. Perhaps you're like me and have a medicine regimen you have to follow. You're dressed and your briefcase or backpack is ready for you to start your work day.

What about your spirit? If your attitude determines your altitude, how high will you fly if you neglect your spirit?

Starting Off

We are made of body, soul, and spirit, and if we do not attend to one, the other two will be negatively affected. If we starve our spirit from the Bread of Life, we will not function as God intends us to. We need to begin our day like Jesus did:

"Now in the morning, having risen a long while before daylight, He went out and departed to a solitary place; and there He prayed."
(Mark 1:35)

The Lord Jesus Christ started His morning in prayer. Perhaps He is on to something? While Jesus is our greatest example of how to be God's man, He wasn't the only person in the Bible who had a consistent devotional life.

Abraham, Jacob, Samuel's parents, King Hezekiah, Job, and David are just some of the Old Testament examples we see of devout believers starting their mornings spending time with God.

How better to begin your day than by reading God's Word and allowing it to mold your mind and prayers?

Would not every day be better if men of God would place the same importance to beginning it with the Lord as David wrote:

"My voice You shall hear in the morning, O Lord; in the morning I will direct it to You, and I will look up." (Psalm 5:3)

We cannot try to go through the day believing our quiet time in the morning will carry us all day any more than we can eat breakfast and not eat again the rest of the day. We need God's Word to sustain us throughout the day.

Setting Out

How many decisions have you made and in hindsight you realize you left God out of the equation? How did that work out for you? I know for me, most of my worst decisions were based solely on what Dave thought. God's Word promises to not only sustain us, but to also prosper us:

"This Book of the Law shall not depart from your mouth, but you shall meditate in it day and night, that you may observe to do according to all that is written in it. For then you will make your way prosperous, and then you will have good success." (Joshua 1:8)

Go back and read the first nine verses of the Book of Joshua. Moses has died and now God is commissioning Joshua to lead His people into the Promise Land.

God promises Joshua that He will hand over the Promised Land to the Israelites; all they have to do is take it. God's only instructions to Joshua are to be strong and of good courage, and to keep his Bible close at hand. If Joshua will not only study God's Word, but also obey it, God promises Joshua great prosperity and success.

Do you think God is just begging us to test Him on this? How badly do you believe our Lord wants to see men of God prosper and succeed in His ways?

How different would our days be if we did? Just imagine you and me leaving our houses and spending our days meditating on and minding God's Word!

How much better of a leader would you be in molding that difficult or deficient employee if you allowed God's Word to lead you?

I am asking all these questions because I want men of God to stop and answer each one of them, imagining how different our lives would be.

Go back to the last five words in Psalm 119:147:

"I hope in Your word."

Throughout the day I place my hope in a lot of things; rarely is it God's Word. That may explain much of my daily anxiety. Too often my day is filled with frustration and failure to meet the goals and expectations I've set for myself. What would those days be like if I relied on God's strength and help? The Bible has the answer:

"Happy is he who has the God of Jacob for his help, whose hope is in the Lord his God." (Psalm 146:5)

The Hebrew word for happy is *asre*, and it means "blessed!, happy!, a heightened state of happiness and joy, implying very favorable circumstances."

This is a level of happiness few men of God experience daily, and yet God's Word promises us such joy. Would not your drive home be quite different if your day was spent in "a heightened state of happiness?"

Of course it would! I drive home and take a different route from the morning purposefully to decompress from the day, and I don't even have that stressful of a job.

However, I want to finish well. When I enter my house, kiss my wife hello, and have dinner with her, I don't want to forget the Lord. I need to go to sleep with Him on my mind and in my heart.

Finishing Up

You no doubt have experienced restless or sleepless nights. Worry is the great thief of peace, and nothing upsets our inner peace more than fatigue. Not getting enough sleep contributes to accidents, mental mistakes and forgetfulness, serious health problems, including depression and premature skin aging, and even causes weight gain.

Men are notorious for keeping things to themselves. There is some wisdom in that. We have to be careful how much of our concerns we share with our wives. We have to be prudent in shielding our brides from unnecessary worry.

Of course, we need to rely on their counsel, but we can be quick to share self-conceived problems. Sometimes we just need to let a situation develop to the end to know the right course to take.

We should always take our concerns to the Lord. When we seek His guidance and strength through prayer and His Word, we find clarity and comfort knowing that nothing surprises God and He is in our corner, no matter the struggle:

"I lay down and slept; I awoke, for the Lord sustained me. I will not be afraid of ten thousands of people who have set themselves against me all around." (Psalm 3:5-6)

Imagine that your son hates you so much that he is trying to kill you. Your own flesh and blood is conspiring and mounting the forces to end your life. Would not that rob you of your sleep?

That is exactly what David was facing when he wrote Psalm 3.

As you read his words, David does not try to pretend he's not concerned. David realized that God knew his heart better than he did. In verse 1, David confessed that he was troubled by Absalom's plotting. However, in verse 3 David writes four important words that as men of God we can never forget:

"But You, O Lord"

We should use those words whenever we are going to acknowledge God's omnipotence, omnipresence, and omniscience. David prefaced his acknowledgment of God's protection with those words. He acknowledged that his strength to carry on came from the Lord.

More importantly in verse 4 of Psalm 3, we read that David took his concerns to the Lord, and God was faithful to hear and comfort him:

"I cried to the Lord with my voice, and He heard me from His holy hill."

God is never too far from us that He will not hear His men cry out to Him. Men of God must never forget that truth. God's man cannot allow pride to keep him from acknowledging his weakness and need for the Heavenly Father's strength.

Let me finish this chapter with a question: if we don't need God's strength, then why did the Apostle Paul tell us to put on the full armor of God?

Turn the page to find the answer…

Chapter Four - Armor Up!

"Therefore take up the whole armor of God, that you may be able to
withstand in the evil day, and having done all, to stand."
(Ephesians 6:13)

As a retired Army First Sergeant who spent 22 years on active
duty, I understand the importance of equipment and training. In
this chapter I want us to focus on three essentials to being God's
man that the whole armor of God provides: *necessity, ability, and
stability.*

Essential #1: Necessity

Without the full armor of God, you will not "be able to withstand
in the evil day." When is the evil day? Men of God know it is the
day in which we live. However, knowledge without action is
worthless. Knowledge with action, applying what we know to be
true, is wisdom.

Putting on the full armor of God isn't just a good idea. The Greek
word for "take up" is *analambano* and gives the impression of
taking something with you with the intent to use.

Paul exhorts us to put on our spiritual armor because he knows
we're going to need it. There is no more sickening feeling than
realizing you forgot something you know you are going to need.

Yet, how many days do we willfully leave our homes without our
spiritual armor, and never even notice or miss it? Some days it is
easy to forget because we are not intentional in being God's man.

When we understand the necessity of the full armor of God, we
will be sure to never leave without it. In Ephesians 6:13, the
Apostle Paul does not make us determine why we need our
armor; he states it clearly.

Dear brother, we live in evil times. The United States as a culture has become what the Prophet Isaiah warned against:

"Woe to those who call evil good, and good evil; who put darkness for light, and light for darkness; who put bitter for sweet, and sweet for bitter!" (Isaiah 5:20)

In America, we call abortion, reproductive rights. We call men crossdressing like women, gender identity. We call homosexuality, an alternative lifestyle. We call illegal aliens, undocumented immigrants. Need I go on?

Who are the ones responsible for this abomination coming to our nation? You can lay the blame at base of the pulpits across America. Too many churches in America are embracing this depravity by heretical teachings on the Bible.

In some cases, churches are outright rejecting the authority of Scripture. God's man has not only abandoned the pulpit, but also in homes across the country.

How this can be, or maybe you're wondering how this happened to you? Heresy happens because we leave ourselves defenseless. Even if we wanted to fight it, on our own we're unable. This is why we need the armor.

Essential #2: Ability

A soldier is confident going into battle for three reasons: his leaders, his equipment, and his training. These three elements are essential for confident combat. Without this combination, the soldier may win, be he will be unnecessarily battered and bloodied.

Element #1: The spiritual warrior has confidence because his leader is King Jesus. We are confident in Jesus because we know He will never abandon us on the battlefield. He left us with this heavenly assurance:

"...and lo, I am with you always, even to the end of the age."
(Matthew 28:20b)

Element #2: The spiritual warrior has confidence because his equipment has all that he needs: truth, righteousness, the gospel of peace, faith, salvation, and most important, the word of God. A spiritual warrior who is not only armored up, but also prayed up, strikes fear in the heart of Satan and his minions. They know they are defeated before they even begin.

Element #3: The spiritual warrior has confidence because he has trained for the day of battle. God's man has walked through the valley of the shadow of death. He has faced many trials and tribulations that have taught him perseverance. Even though he has experienced weariness, he knows the effort is for his gain and God's glory:

"And let us not grow weary while doing good, for in due season we shall reap if we do not lose heart." (Galatians 6:9)

If God's man follows King Jesus, daily puts on his spiritual armor, and is constantly training through discipleship, then he will be a man on whom you can count. He will be stable and not waver.

Essential #3: Stability

God's man does not crumble under pressure; in fact, he leads a life that is mostly stress-free. A stress-free life does not mean there are no stressors. Life comes at us with stressors. The stress-free life comes with knowing how to deal with those stressors.

My youngest daughter Becky called me one morning when she was in college all stressed out about an exam.

I told her to not stress about it. I told if the issue she was stressing about was out of her control to not stress about it. I also told her that if it was under her control, to not stress about it. She was curious at how that was possible and said she knew I was about to teach her a life lesson.

This lesson is for all of us: if a stressful situation is under our control, then seek God's guidance and deal with it. If it is beyond our control, give it to God and trust Him with it. Pretty simple, right? Remember, simple rarely means easy. We have to learn to trust God, especially in life situations beyond our control.

We can do that when we take up "the shield of faith with which you will be able to quench all the fiery darts of the wicked one." Satan delights in men crumbling under pressure. If I claim to be God's man and yet fall apart whenever stressors come my way that is when Satan's mocking becomes the loudest.

There's an old saying that says a Bible that is falling apart is owned by a life that isn't. Why is that and what does it have to do with being a stable man? How did the Apostle Paul describe the word of God in his letter to the Ephesians? He called it the sword of the Spirit. The only offensive weapon we have in our spiritual armor is God's Word.

The problem is too many men put on their armor but leave their sword where they left it when they got home from church on Sunday. God's man without his sword, even with the rest of his equipment, is unarmed. Oh, he can defend himself somewhat, but primarily he will take a beating all day without ever returning a heavenly blow back at the devil.

The lesson I shared earlier from my pastor is a good reminder in this case: always turn to Jesus for our example. Go and read again for the first time in Luke 4:1-13 where Jesus is tempted by Satan. How does Christ respond to Satan's three attempts at tempting Him? He replies, "It is written." On his final attempt, Satan even quotes Scripture to Christ, and yet our Lord responded the same.

Jesus battled Satan with the word of God, the sword of the Spirit, and so should we.

We cannot read a five-minute devotion, turn on Christian radio and listen to a sermon or Bible teaching and believe we are being discipled. That is known as spiritual milk.

God's man needs spiritual meat and that means becoming a student of the Bible.

Don't quit on me now! In the next chapter I have a simple three-step checklist to follow...

Chapter Five - Study Up!

"All Scripture is given by inspiration of God, and is profitable for doctrine, for reproof, for correction, for instruction in righteousness, that the man of God may be complete, thoroughly equipped for every good work."
(2 Timothy 3:16-17)

Verses 10-17 in Paul's second letter to his protégé and spiritual son, Timothy, have the subtitle of "The Man of God and the Word of God." History tells us that Stephen Langton, an Archbishop of Canterbury, around AD 1227 put the chapter divisions in the Bible we use today. I do not know if he was responsible for the subtitles, but whoever was I tip my hat to them on this one.

Random House Dictionary defines the conjunctional use of *and* as "along or together with; as well as; in addition to; besides; also; moreover." You're probably shaking your head right now not believing I felt the need to define such a simple word. If you're the man who picks up his Bible on Sunday from where he left it the previous Sunday, then yes, you need this lesson.

God's man is not complete without God's Word. If I was to take a poll of you reading this right now, I would guess this discipline is one of your greatest weaknesses, second only to purity.

Life tends to get in the way of what man needs most. Our workaday world competes for every second we have. If we do not set aside time with the steadfast intention to get into God's Word daily, then we will spiritually starve ourselves.

I like checklists. A checklist is a wonderful way to stay on task and to finish what you started. Let's call this checklist, *The Three L's of Bible Study.*

This is more of a roadmap to becoming more connected to God's Word than it is a how-to study your Bibles.

This checklist gives us a systematic way to become better Bible students. The three L's are *learn, live,* and *love.* This system is most difficult when you begin but gets easier as you go. It will become second nature to you.

Step 1: Learn

I once had a really stupid idea for an invention. I was going to come up with a really inexpensive gadget that you could buy at the sales counter at your local Christian book store, for $4.99. It was a Bible meter. Talk about stupid! Who wants to be reminded how little they read their Bible? It would be similar to the dusty weight scale in your bathroom.

Seriously, the idea is wrong because it is the wrong approach to reading God's Word. God's man needs to understand the value of being discipled through Scripture. There are plenty of excellent Bible reading plans, but I'm going to give you a simple one that is easy to follow. I taught this to my children.

There are 31 proverbs and 150 psalms in the Old Testament. That means you can read one proverb and five psalms every day. Read Proverbs 1 and Psalms 1-5 on the 1st day of the month, Proverbs 2 and Psalms 6-10 on the 2nd, and so on. If you did this for one year, only this, your walk with Christ would be unrecognizable from when you began. You would be amazed. *(There's an actual daily checklist you can follow in Chapter 12)*

I remember when my late son Sergeant Eddie Jeffers (he was killed in Iraq on September 19, 2007) and I were talking about a book I had sent him. It was written by the lead singer of Casting Crowns, Mark Hall. The book is titled *Lifestories: Finding God's "Voice of Truth" Through Everyday Life*; I highly recommend it.

Eddie told me that he couldn't relate to Mark's life and depth of spirituality. I responded that Mark's life is so much different from Eddie's. He doesn't get up in the morning wondering if this is his last day on earth.

Eddie told me, "Most days Dad, I just read the proverb and psalms of the day as you taught me, pray to God asking Him to keep my soldiers and me alive, and to not dishonor Him."

I was silent for a moment, and then I said, "Eddie, if all Christians in our country did just that, America would be so different than it is today."

Imagine if every man of God did just that. If every man who confesses Christ as his Lord would read just one proverb and five psalms every day, how would that change him? How would that change his family? How would that change his church? How would that change his community? How would that change the state where he lives? How would that change America?

My dear brother-in-Christ, you and I, if we are to be the spiritual leaders of our homes and spiritual warriors in our culture, then we *must* hone our skills with the sword of the Spirit.

The Apostle Paul told Timothy that "all Scripture is...profitable for doctrine..." The Greek word translated for doctrine is *didaskalia* and it simply means "teaching, instruction."

Scripture is where we learn God's precepts and principles. A precept is a rule by which we are to live. A principle, in the biblical sense, is a fundamental truth; it is the foundation of our belief system. This is where many nonbelievers err about the Bible. They believe it's just a book of rules written by men.

They are half right. The rules, precepts and principles, bring us God's protection and provision. To know how God wants us to live, we must first learn His plan for our lives. We do so through the daily discipline of studying God's Word.

How can we know that the Bible is true? That comes from the second benefit Paul describes to Timothy: reproof. The Greek word translated for reproof is *elegchos*. It means "a proof, that by which a thing is proved or tested; conviction."

Man of God, when you read Scripture and allow the Holy Spirit to illuminate its Truth, the doctrine you are learning is proved in your heart. When that happens, you will begin to live its truth.

Step 2: Live

What is your greatest desire as God's man? A better question would be what is God's great desire for us? Go back to the cross. Jesus paid the price for our sins so that we may be right with God the Father through Him:

"Therefore, as through one man's offense judgment came to all men, resulting in condemnation, even so through one Man's righteous act the free gift came to all men, resulting in justification of life. For as by one man's disobedience many were made sinners, so also by one Man's obedience many will be made righteous." (Romans 5:18-19)

I can never repay Jesus for assuming my sin debt. Whenever we receive a gift of grace, a gift that we did not deserve, and a gift we definitely could not afford, there should be a heart of gratitude. The greatest way I show gratitude to my Savior is through faith and obedience.

The more I learn about Jesus, the more I begin to live my life for Him. When I fail, I can go to the Bible to receive correction. The Greek word for correction in 2 Timothy 3:16 is *epanorthosis*, and it means "restoration to an upright state; correction, improvement of character." Is not improvement of character what every man of God should be seeking? If you answered yes, then brother open your Bible and start reading.

If your back just stiffened and all kinds of excuses started running through your mind, I hear you. To overcome this rebellious spirit within us, we must purpose in our hearts that we want to improve our characters so that we can truly be God's men. If I am going to live by God's Word, I have to learn it.

There's a great reward found in 2 Timothy 3:16 for the man who will set his heart upon studying Scripture. Paul ends the verse reminding us that Scripture is "for instruction in righteousness." What type of instruction? The kind you expect your children to receive when you send them to school or homeschool them.

You want your children to receive an education that will serve them in life. That is one use of the word instruction. The other use, which is relevant to our discussion, the Blue Letter Bible website defines as "whatever in adults also cultivates the soul, especially by correcting mistakes and curbing passions."

Are you a quick-tempered man? Read your Bible! Are you viewing pornography on the internet? Read your Bible instead! Brother, if you want to grow in biblical virtue, how do you expect to do that outside of reading your Bible?

Reading your Bible is not hard work; it is heart work. In 2 Timothy 3:17, Paul gives us a taste of what awaits us if we will live our lives in the light of Scripture. We will become complete, meaning perfect in the biblical sense. Every good work that God has designed us for, He will equip us.

I have hated who I've been in the past; loathing my sins and failures, knowing that God expects and deserves so much more from me. I hated the life I had lived knowing that I should love the life of being a Christian man. It wasn't until I began starting my days bathing in Scripture, that I began living the life I knew God intended for me. Once I started to do that, my loathing turned to loving. Loving life, loving my wife, loving my family, loving my church, and most importantly, loving God.

Step 3: Love

As much as I have wanted and want to be God's man, to love Him as Jesus instructed us to in the Greatest Commandment, I know God desires it more. He wants to love me abundantly and to have strong fellowship with me.

God wants me to be His man and to walk in His ways. He knows the plans He has for me and how He wants to prosper me, to paraphrase the Prophet Jeremiah. Asaph the psalmist gives some insight into God's desire for me:

"Oh, that My people would listen to Me, that Israel would walk in My ways! I would soon subdue their enemies." (Psalm 81:13-14)

God not only wants me to love Him and walk in His ways, He wants all men to do so. America looks to every way possible to subdue our enemies, and all this time God long ago promised to do so if we would just listen to Him.

As we study and live God's Word, we grow in our love for Him and His ways. We desire only to please our Heavenly Father and to spend time with Him. Our love grows for God through our love for His Son. Love for God is how we see God.

So many skeptics say they would believe in God if they could just see Him. That is not how it works; God doesn't succumb to our demands. We come to Him in faith, and it is through that faith that we find God and finally see Him because He lives in us:

"Whoever confesses that Jesus is the Son of God, God abides in him, and he in God. And we have known and believed the love that God has for us. God is love, and he who abides in love abides in God, and God in him." (1 John 4:15-16)

To be God's man, we must come to the full realization that He has thought of everything we need to fulfill His purpose for our lives: "thoroughly equipped for every good work."

God hasn't left anything out, or overlooked something important. All we need to be God's man is found in His Word, and more importantly, is found in Him.

All we have to do is look to Him; better yet, look *up* to Him...

Chapter Six - Look Up!

"My voice You shall hear in the morning, O Lord; in the morning I
will direct it to You, and I will look up."
(Psalm 5:3)

On a scale of 1 to 10, with 1 being weakest and 10 being
strongest, how would you grade your fellowship with Jesus?
How aware are you daily of His presence? Does the Lord only
hear from you when you're freaking out, or do you have regular
conversations with the King of kings?

Too often we spend our days looking at all the chaos and
confusion around us, and rarely do we look to heaven for calm
and comfort. The world in which we live can be turbulent, but
the world that awaits us is one of tranquility.

There are days when I wish the Lord would take me home, but
often times I cause my own anxiety by focusing on the earthly
instead of eternity.

How do I deliberately go through the day with my focus on Jesus
and His vision for my life? How does God's man "press toward
the goal for the prize of the upward call of God in Christ Jesus" of
which Paul wrote to the Philippian church?

The Bible gives three mental states that God's man needs to
ingrain into his character to constantly keep his eye on the prize:
desire, determination, and diligence.

Mental State #1: Desire

Before we can go on, I need you to do something. This must be
an actual exercise and not just a mental image you conjure up.
Get a notepad or piece of paper and write down your greatest
ambition as God's man. Write down the first thing that comes to
mind. Please don't write down what you think would sound
good.

If this is going to be of any use to you, you must earnestly seek your heart and find your greatest ambition as God's man. If nothing comes up, then write down *nothing*. That may seem counter to what you're trying to accomplish here, but you have to have a starting point to go forward.

I will share with you my greatest desire that God gave me through His Word. I will never forget this moment. I was stationed in Germany, had yet to marry my bride Karen. It was a beautiful summer afternoon in June of 1997, one of those rare, amazing summer days.

I lived on the bottom floor in my apartment building and I had my windows open enjoying the breeze. I was reading through my Bible, using a read through the Bible study guide, and that day's Old Testament reading was 2 Chronicles 1. Solomon has become king at a very young age. It is estimated that he became king between the ages of 12 to 20.

We read in verse 7 that God appears to Solomon at night and says to him, "Ask! What shall I give you?"

Imagine yourself at that age and God is giving you the proverbial magic genie lamp, or so you might think. In our immaturity we may ask for earthly things, and yet that doesn't enter Solomon's mind. Instead of material things, Solomon asks for wisdom and knowledge.

In verses 11 and 12, God is delighted with Solomon's response and he grants Solomon not only wisdom and knowledge, but He also gives him "riches and honor, such as none of the kings have had who were before you, nor shall any after you have the like."

I remember the Holy Spirit nearly physically pushing me on my shoulder to get on my face before God and ask Him for wisdom and knowledge. My desire for that was not so God would also grant me wishes. I had never before wanted something as badly as I wanted godly wisdom and knowledge.

I found myself face down on my rug pleading and weeping to God for what Solomon had desired. It was one of the most important spiritual moments in my life, before and since.

God began showing me things in the Bible that I had missed before. My hunger for His word, to understand it and implement it in my life, was almost insatiable. As I write this, I realize that since that time I have too often strayed from that desire.

My life verse is the result of that desire that God gave me on that summer day in 1997. I have embraced what David wrote in one of his psalms:

"Delight yourself also in the Lord, and He shall give you the desires of your heart." (Psalm 37:4)

This great desire that God gave me evolved into a drive that I had never before experienced, and as a senior noncommissioned officer in the United States Army, I knew a lot about the subject. My desire to be God's man through gaining wisdom and knowledge gave me a new purpose in life. I was determined to not let God down.

Mental State 2: Determination

God's man is going to face challenges, even persecution. If he is not, then it is highly doubtful he is consistently on the frontlines of the spiritual battle we discussed in Chapter 4. One of the greatest characteristics that God's man must develop is determination, or steadfastness. My pastor describes it as stickability. God's man cannot be a quitter!

The need for dogged determination may be simple to understand, but it is rarely easy to maintain. This is why, particularly in the New Testament, you read exhortations to remain steadfast. One such urging is found in Paul's first letter to the Corinthian church:

"Therefore, my beloved brethren, be steadfast, immovable, always abounding in the work of the Lord, knowing that your labor is not in vain in the Lord." (1 Corinthians 15:58)

If you want to know what Corinth was like, imagine the debauchery of New Orleans. If you want to know the state of the Corinthian church, just imagine the typical apostate church in America today. Both were a hot mess!

How did Corinth and America get into the messes in which they find themselves? Instead of affecting their cultures, both past and present, churches allow the culture to affect them. When we defile the body of Christ by allowing sin to run rampant, both within and without the walls, then all hell literally breaks loose.

The same ailment can affect each of us individually. This may not seem like any special revelation, because it's not. However, it is such a common problem that God's man needs to understand how to prevent and protect him and his family from this illness.

Paul gives the remedy near the end of his letter in the verse above. To be steadfast literally means to be *immovable.* Paul is emphatic that we cannot be swayed by sin nor can we allow it. The Greek for immovable is *ametakinētos*, and it metaphorically means to "be firmly persistent." It literally means to "be unmoved." God's man is not giving into sin nor is he tolerating it.

If Paul had ended there, I might be prone to say to him, "Easier said than done." Paul knew something about steadfastness and overcoming temptation; remember Romans 7?

Paul admonishes us to be "always abounding in the work of the Lord." The Greek for abounding is *perisseuō*, it relates to "a thing which comes in abundance, or overflows unto one, something falls to the lot of one in large measure."

Paul is telling us that our work for the Lord should encompass every aspect of our lives.

If it is my heart's desire to always "be about my Father's business," as our Lord Jesus was, then that desire will grow into a steely steadfastness. It will not only result in my work for the Lord in my church, but also, and just as important, in my home, my neighborhood, and in my employment.

Dear brother, this type of determination is not the type you see in workaholics. Random House Dictionary defines *workaholic* as "a person who works compulsively at the expense of other pursuits." In other words, this person is avoiding other responsibilities, usually his or her family. This ailment afflicts men primarily and it is a failure of God's man being the husband, father, and Christian brother we are called to be.

The true heart's desire to be God's man results in a determination to do what God has shown you. You may not be able to imagine your life getting any busier. I promise you brother that you won't feel busy; you will feel blessed. You will feel your heart swell with joy, knowing that your determination has not only resulted in doing the Lord's work, but also it has brought about the discipline you have so desperately sought.

Mental State #3: Discipline

By discipline, I mean a spiritual maturity and stickability that comes through discipleship. The product is that of which Peter wrote in his second letter:

"But also for this very reason, giving all diligence, add to your faith virtue, to virtue knowledge, to knowledge self-control, to self-control perseverance, to perseverance godliness, to godliness brotherly kindness, and to brotherly kindness love. For if these things are yours and abound, you will be neither barren nor unfruitful in the knowledge of our Lord Jesus Christ." (2 Peter 1:5-8)

I want to closely examine each characteristic Peter lists in verses 5-7 to help us understand the totality of what is possible.

The Greek word for faith is *pistis*, and it is more than trusting God. In general, this faith a strong belief in the truth; it becomes a conviction. Specifically, as described in the Blue Letter Bible, it is "the conviction that God exists and is the creator and ruler of all things." Furthermore, faith in Jesus Christ is "a strong and welcome conviction or belief that Jesus is the Messiah, through whom we obtain eternal salvation." Is this your faith?

Following faith is virtue. The Random House Dictionary defines virtue as "moral excellence; goodness; righteousness." It closely aligns to the Greek *aretē* translated virtue. Virtue is not just moral goodness; it is "a virtuous course of thought, feeling and action." Biblical virtue results in the humility and purity that God's man seeks.

Biblical virtue leads to biblical knowledge. The knowledge Peter wrote of is the general understanding of the word, simply intelligence. Biblically it is "the general knowledge of religion." The Greek word is *gnosis* and it is where we derive the English word *gnostic*. Gnosticism became the enemy of true Christian faith and over the centuries resulted in the Unitarian and Universalist belief systems. Knowledge improperly applied can become an idol, even to the point of a false religion or cult.

The type of knowledge Peter exhorts leads us to self-control. How many of us could use more self-control? The King James Version renders the Greek *egkrateia* as temperance, which gives the idea of someone who has mastered his desires and passions; particularly "sensual appetites." Perhaps you struggle in this area. If you're trying to get to this point in your walk with Christ by skipping the first three characteristics Peter outlined, you may have discovered why you keep failing. It is also why you keep quitting.

However, true self-control leads to perseverance, the stickability we are seeking. This is godly patience; it means you are not a quitter. You are constant and steadfast in your walk with Christ.

The Blue Letter Bible defines the Greek *hypomonē*: "the characteristic of a man who is not swerved from his deliberate purpose and his loyalty to faith and piety by even the greatest trials and sufferings."

Serving the Lord is not for the fainthearted. This is why the old adage of "be careful of praying for patience; God just may answer that prayer" is so true. Perseverance is God's prayer for us because it molds us into whom God has designed us to be.

This strength of character leads us to the next characteristic Peter outlines: godliness. It means exactly what we think it means when we think of godliness. It is awe and reverence before God, such that we live righteous lives.

Philadelphia is known as "the city of brotherly love," a misnomer to many who have visited that city. However, *philadelphia* is the Greek word transliterated in 2 Peter 1:7 as "brotherly kindness." It is the love that Christians are called to have for one another. It is the type of Christian behavior Paul writes of Romans:

"Be kindly affectionate to one another with brotherly love, in honor giving preference to one another." (Romans 12:10)

This type of love results in a sweet fellowship that can only be experienced between followers of Jesus Christ. It is not something to which you naturally attain. It is brought by the empowering of the Holy Spirit through the grace and mercy in our lives overflowing to others. It leads to the final thing: unconditional love.

This Greek word is no doubt familiar to most Christians: *agape*. We know of agape love because so many ministries include this word in their titles. The King James Version renders the Greek as *charity*. It is a benevolent affection that leads to good will. This love drives me to evangelism and service to others.

This all leads to the fruitful and productive lives that God's man is called to live. Go back to the question I asked at the beginning of this chapter: On a scale of 1 to 10, with 1 being weakest and 10 being strongest, how would you grade your fellowship with Jesus?

I encourage you to apply that grading scale to each of the eight characteristics Peter wrote of in his second letter. This exercise will show you where you need to grow in your walk with Christ.

However, God's man might think it would be enough to study his Bible and apply this grading scale of godly characteristics we've discussed. It would definitely bring improvement, but it would not get you to the level of walking with the Lord that we should all desire. It takes something more; something much more important. It takes a prayer life that is greater and more fulfilling than your mind can imagine or your heart can desire.

Time to get on our knees...

Chapter Seven - Pray Up!

"Evening and morning and at noon I will pray, and cry aloud,
and He shall hear my voice." (Psalm 55:17)

As I write this, yesterday was Mother's Day 2018. I thought about how long it had been since my mother (July 2000) and my father (August 2004) went to be with Jesus. My parents were by no means the godliest parents. In fact, they divorced when I was just a teenager. Nevertheless, I sorely miss talking with them.

My father and I had an estranged relationship for over 20 years until God had me reach out to my father and restore our relationship. I cherished the last seven years we had together.

As I thought about that, the Holy Spirit reminded me how often I go without speaking to my Heavenly Father. If I so long to speak with my earthly parents, then why do I starve myself of the sweet communication with God continuously available to me? I tend to forget that God is always ready to hear from me.

When you take the verse at the beginning of this chapter out of context, it sure would make a great refrigerator magnet or paper weight. By itself it is good news. However, in context of David's psalm, it is even better news. The title heading for Psalm 55 is "Trust in God Concerning the Treachery of Friends."

David wrote this while being threatened by a conspiracy headed by one of his former friends. This conspiracy was hatched in Jerusalem while David was king and it caused great confusion. No one could be sure who to trust. David turned to the One who he knew he could trust. David talked to God daily.

God's man needs to have a devotional life that is one of prayerfulness. Such a life is possible by three intentional steps we should take every day: talk, test, and trust.

Step #1: Talk

Very early in the Bible we see man talking with God. Many times in the Old Testament prayer is described as calling "on the name of the LORD." We see this with Adam's son Seth and his son:

"And as for Seth, to him also a son was born; and he named him Enosh. Then men began to call on the name of the Lord."
(Genesis 4:26)

The Bible doesn't tell us what caused Seth and Enosh to pray, but I imagine that Adam imparted the importance of talking with God to his son. Adam was uniquely qualified to explain what sin can bring to a family. His original sin got him and his wife Eve kicked out of the Garden of Eden. Sin caused Seth's older brother Cain to kill another brother Abel, whom Seth never met. It would have been wise for Adam to teach his new son how to pray.

If God's man is to be intentional about talking with God, then he will have to set aside time. David wrote in Psalm 55 that he would pray "evening and morning and at noon." Whether David actually prayed three times a day or he meant that he prayed throughout the day is not the point. David purposefully talked with God.

Why? David knew that God was waiting to hear from him and that his Heavenly Father would hear him. Sometimes it is easy for God's man to doubt whether or not God hears our prayers. However, if we are in the habit of talking with God daily, then our confidence in His hearing us grows with each passing day. God's man is a habitual pray-er!

The New Testament gives an example of a man who was not a follower of Jesus Christ who nevertheless was very devout, helped the poor, "and prayed to God." This man taught his family to fear God. His name was Cornelius, a centurion in the Italian Regiment. You can read about Cornelius and his meeting with the Apostle Peter in Acts 10.

What is instructive to us is that Cornelius' steadfastness in prayer led him to an encounter with one of the followers of Jesus Christ. If this man, who feared God and yet was not a follower of God's only begotten Son, knew to pray to God, how much more should we who call ourselves Christians do so?

Old habits are hard to break. If you are stuck in a rut of prayerlessness, you may be thinking right now that you just don't have time to have such a devotional life. Your schedule is too full and you can't manage another undertaking.

The truth is you cannot afford not to make prayer a priority in your life. How can a follower of Christ not speak to the One he follows? How can God's man not talk daily with God? Your schedule is too full and life is too hectic *because* you are not starting out and sustaining throughout the day intentionally praying.

Every decision we make, be it small or large, private, personal, or professional, should be bathed in prayer. Sometimes a decision comes upon you quickly and you only have time for "a quick shower." What is better, no prayer, or a quick prayer seeking God's guidance?

If you're having a hard time seeing the benefit of making prayerfulness a priority in your life, why not give it a try? What do you have to lose?

Set aside some time and call out to God for guidance and wisdom, and see what happens. God is up to the test.

Step #2: Test

For clarity, let's be sure we understand what I mean by testing God. I am not talking about trying to manipulate God with prayers that begin with, "If you love me God, then you will..." or "If you truly are a loving God, then you will..." I hope that is clear.

God has promised to answer prayer. Even if you consider yourself the lowliest among the lowly, God will hear your prayer and answer it:

"He shall regard the prayer of the destitute, and shall not despise their prayer." (Psalm 102:17)

One of the prayer promises we find in the New Testament that is often abused by the "Name It and Claim It" false teachers so prevalent today on Christian radio and television comes from Jesus. The last night on earth, Jesus promised His disciples that, "If you ask anything in My name, I will do it."

Today's peddlers of Christ will tell you that all you have to do is ask in Jesus' name, believe He will do it, and it will happen. They almost act as though Jesus is some magic genie lamp who will give us unlimited wishes.

This is a conditional request that we make. If I may expound on Christ's statement, it would be, "If you ask anything in my name, if it is for your good, and appropriate to your character, I will do it." Christ is not going to fulfill our idolatrous or lustful desires, no matter how much we believe He will or call on His name.

An example of righteous prayer comes from the followers of the early church when Peter was imprisoned by King Herod. Herod had the Apostle James beheaded, and because this pleased the Jews, he had Peter arrested. Peter's brothers and sisters in Christ all prayed for him:

"Peter was therefore kept in prison, but constant prayer was offered to God for him by the church. And when Herod was about to bring him out, that night Peter was sleeping, bound with two chains between two soldiers; and the guards before the door were keeping the prison."
(Acts 12:5-6)

If you don't know how the story ends, you'll want to read Acts 12:1-19 and see how God was faithful to answer faithful prayers.

What you will find is one of the first prayer meetings recorded in the New Testament where intercessory prayer was lifted up to God. It would take a miracle for Peter to be saved from the grip of an evil king, and indeed a miracle happened.

God is faithful to answer our prayers as He sees fit. When we test God's promises about prayer, we are confirming and proving that He is a faithful and loving God. He is worthy of our trust.

Step #3: Trust

How much do you trust God? The last section we just covered was on testing God. Let's each test our trust in God. Take a moment to write down one issue you are dealing with right now, an issue that has you concerned about its outcome.

No doubt you have considered many options of how to deal with the issue. You may have already prayed about it. Underline the issue you've listed, and below it, write down those options. Is one of them giving it to the Lord? Perhaps you believe you are trusting God in this area, but if you haven't released it to the Lord, then how much are you really trusting Him?

I am not talking about foregoing your responsibilities in this issue. I am talking about allowing the outcome to be determined by God. If we are truly trusting God, we will be confident in how the future turns out. You will know your confidence in the Lord is strong because you will have a peace about your issue:

"You will keep him in perfect peace, whose mind is stayed on You, because he trusts in You. Trust in the Lord forever, for in YAH, the Lord, is everlasting strength." (Isaiah 26:3-4)

The phrase "in perfect peace" is transliterated from the Hebrew word *shalowm*, or the more familiar spelling, *shalom*. In the original text it is written, *shalowm shalowm*.

The Blue Letter Bible tells us this word has multiple meanings in the Hebrew language: *peace, well, peaceably, welfare, salute, prosperity, did, safe, health, peaceable.* Its usage can mean "completeness (in number); safety, soundness (in body); welfare, health, prosperity; peace, quiet, tranquility, contentment; peace, friendship (with humans and with God); peace (from war). "

Does your trust in God include such perfect peace? Are you resting in perfect peace? If the answer is no, it is probably because you haven't really prayed about it in the way you need to arrive to such a peaceful state of mind.

Sending a shotgun prayer request up to heaven for God to deal with this issue is not going to get you there. Too often we go through the motions of seeking God's help, and then we continue to try to engineer the outcome in our own strength or through others:

"It is better to trust in the Lord than to put confidence in man."
(Psalm 118:8)

Fear of the unknown can be crippling. Fear can cause God's man to make rash decisions, forgetting he is a child of Almighty God, the maker and sustainer of all things. We habitually trust in our own abilities and those of others. So often, we look at the "facts" before us and believe we have all the information we need to act.

Dear brother, if you have excluded God from the analysis, then your decision is based on incomplete intelligence. In other words, you need to know "the rest of the story." Even if it seems that a multitude is set against you, God's man can declare:

"Though an army may encamp against me, my heart shall not fear; though war may rise against me, in this I will be confident."
(Psalm 27:3)

What is the "this" in which King David is placing his confidence? If you read all of Psalm 27, you will see that David is praying a prayer of confidence to God. David knows that God will triumph over his enemies. David is going to rely on God instead of his own abilities or that of his armies. Notice at the end of the psalm how David exhorts his own faith to be faithful:

"Wait on the Lord; be of good courage, and He shall strengthen your heart; wait, I say, on the Lord!" (Psalm 27:14)

David's level of confidence in God did not come solely from his experience and knowledge of God. Psalm 27 is titled, "An Exuberant Declaration of Faith," a declaration made possible from an intimate relationship with the One in whom David had faith. Faith is simply trusting God!

Do you *trust* God? More importantly, have you trusted Jesus Christ for your salvation? Have you come to realize that your sinfulness cannot be overcome by anything you do or do not do? Have you confessed your sins to Christ, sought His forgiveness, and accepted His atoning sacrifice on the cross?

If not, that is the first real act of faith you will take in this journey of becoming God's man. You must trust Christ as your personal Lord and Savior before you can trust Him with anything else.

Whether you've just now trusted Christ, or you have been a follower of His for some time now, one thing that should be happening is clarity of mind. Another way of saying this is, "Clearing up the stinking thinking."

A habitual life of prayerfulness and studying God's Word brings this clarity of mind. Turn the page to see how...

Chapter Eight - Sober Up!

"Therefore gird up the loins of your mind, be sober, and rest your hope fully upon the grace that is to be brought to you at the revelation of Jesus Christ." (1 Peter 1:13)

For those of you who partake in beverage alcohol, this chapter is not addressed to drinking. While I personally believe, and can make the biblical case for abstaining, that is another book for another time.

With the amount and consistency of blasphemous and heretical teachings coming from those who claim to be ministers and experts of God's Word, it can be difficult to navigate the waters of Truth. How does God's man clear up the stinking thinking that so easily ensnares American society?

Psalm 119 is titled, "Meditation on the Excellencies of the Word of God." The use of the word *excellencies* in the title denotes preeminence. Random House Dictionary defines *preeminence* as "distinguished above or before others; superior; surpassing." The psalmist makes the case for the supremacy of God's Word.

I want you to stop and read all of Psalm 119. This will help set the tone for this chapter. Go ahead; it will take you some time, but I'll wait.

Did you read it all? As I was reading it, I couldn't help but recognize many of my struggles in life and supplications to God. One of the first Bible verses I remember as a child is Psalm 119:105:

"Your word is a lamp to my feet and a light to my path."

Growing up, on Sunday mornings I used to watch a religious show on CBS titled, "Lamp Unto My Feet." I remember many famous actors performing scenes that taught moral and religious lessons. Unfortunately, CBS cancelled it in 1978.

Even before I was saved in 1981, that show had a profound impact on my life. Growing up a Catholic, I learned many lessons on right and wrong, and how I was supposed to live my life. Nevertheless, the many choices I made as a teenager and young adult were very destructive. I had a self-constructed life philosophy that was part Bible and mostly of the world.

It wasn't until I began reading my Bible in earnest that I started discovering the Truth. First, it showed me the way to salvation. Then I began, and am still to this day, learning God's plan for my life. The most excellent thing about God's Word is that it brings clarity of mind. I become most frustrated when things are confusing and muddled. The Bible clears all that up.

In this chapter's verse, the Apostle Peter is showing God's man how he is to live for God because we are His children. Peter writes in verse 4 that we have "an inheritance incorruptible and undefiled and does not fade away."

Peter bridges verse 3-12 with the word *therefore*. In verse 13, we find three spiritual benefits from our heavenly inheritance: spiritual mind, spiritual soberness, and spiritual hope.

Benefit #1: Spiritual Mind

The more I read Scripture, the more I change my mind about things. I'm not saying I am double-minded. I'm saying I change my mind often in the light of Scripture.

That is a good thing! In my sinful nature, my mind will dwell on worldly things. Without a daily dose of Bible reading, my flesh will take over my spirit and soul. All the beneficial things Paul tells the Philippian church to mediate on in chapter 4, verse 8 will be ignored and I will dwell on earthly matters.

Paul told the Christians in Rome that is not how it has to be:

"For those who live according to the flesh set their minds on the things of the flesh, but those who live according to the Spirit, the things of the Spirit. For to be carnally minded is death, but to be spiritually minded is life and peace." (Romans 8:5-6)

How many times have you heard people say they wanted peace of mind? Are not most of us seeking peaceful lives? While we may not be able to control the external forces in life, we can control our attitude towards them.

Whenever I teach leadership classes, one of the first things I try to get across to my audience is that their response is always their own. In other words, no matter what is happening around us, we have control over how we respond to events.

Our minds are very powerful and the old adage "mind over matter" has a lot of truth to it. I may not be able to always control what comes into my mind, but I can control on what it dwells.

What is a spiritual mind? The Bible gives a simple definition: it is the mind of Christ. In Romans 8:6, Paul describes two types of minds: carnal and spiritual.

The Greek word for carnal is *sarx* and it can refer to the flesh (what covers a living creature), the actual body, or a living creature. The fourth usage is how it is used by Paul in Romans 8:6; it is translated flesh, but this time it speaks of our human nature, one that is apart from divine influence. It is simply, our sinful nature.

The Greek word for spiritual is *pneuma*, and this can refer to the Holy Spirit, the spirit referring to our souls, the center of our emotions, or it can even refer to angelic beings, heavenly spirits. The Blue Letter Bible gives the essence of its usage in Romans 8:6: "the spiritual nature of Christ, higher than the highest angels and equal to God, the divine nature of Christ."

In other words, the mind of Christ.

This mind is one of which God's man need never to be ashamed. It is a mind that is acceptable to God. It is a mind that has biblical truth and wisdom in control about what we think. It is a humble mind, one willing to acquiesce to others. It is one that is sober.

Benefit #2: Spiritual Soberness

A spiritually sober man is a calm man, one not easily given to "going off" all the time. I confess this is one of my greatest spiritual struggles. This weakness does not have to define me.

Peter instructs us to be sober because of our heavenly inheritance. The Greek word for sober is *nepho*, and it denotes a "calm and collected spirit." It also gives the sense of watchfulness and discretion.

God's man thinks things through, and he does so because he is bathed in God's Word. God's man takes biblical knowledge and allows the Holy Spirit to reveal biblical wisdom:

"You, through Your commandments, make me wiser than my enemies; for they are ever with me. I have more understanding than all my teachers, for Your testimonies are my meditation."
(Psalm 119:98-99)

There are two young brothers-in-Christ in my life that display wisdom beyond their years. The first one is our Associate Pastor of Students and Evangelism, Andrew Bosak.

I had the great privilege of watching Brother Andrew grow up in his teen years and seeing God call him to the ministry.

Brother Andrew's history degree and master of divinity give him a unique insight to both mankind and Scripture. He preaches well beyond his years.

While Andrew is gifted in preaching, it is his discernment that is most noticeable.

He is slow to speak, and always mindful of who he is and how to conduct himself. It is a spiritual soberness borne out of his love for Christ. His passion for Christ and for us to bear Christlikeness is always present in his preaching.

This discernment is also present in the second young man, Steve Deace (it rhymes with pace). Steve was not raised in the church and did not become a Christian until his 30's. He lived a pagan lifestyle and was radically changed by the gospel.

Steve hosts a television show on Conservative Review TV and a podcast on Westwood One Radio (broadcasted live on Blaze TV). As a close friend of mine, Steve has taught me much in how to apply biblical wisdom in the arena of politics. Steve's ability to quickly discern how the Bible applies to almost any issue in our culture is something to behold.

Both men are spiritually sober. They look at life through a biblical lens. It is their biblical worldviews that guide their words and actions. It is how God's man is to conduct himself.

A man who is spiritually minded and sober, being watchful, is one who isn't prone to despair. God's man understands that even when the world seems to be falling apart, God is still in control.

God's man is spiritually hopeful.

Benefit #3: Spiritual Hope

How long has the American church misplaced its hope in man instead of God? I confess I have at times given into the false choice of we have to trust the G-O-P instead of G-O-D.

My pastor Brother Dennis once shared this interesting insight with me. Organizations such as Focus on the Family, the Family Research Council, and National Right to Life are nothing more than parachurch entities.

They are trying to do the job of the church. Too often they carry the Republican Party's water instead of carrying the banner of Jesus Christ.

I cannot count how many times my elected representatives have disappointed me by not standing in the gap for God. My disappointment comes from my misplaced hope in man. The Apostle Paul wrote of a hope that does not disappoint:

"Now hope does not disappoint, because the love of God has been poured out in our hearts by the Holy Spirit who was given to us."
(Romans 5:5)

We become fainthearted because we allow our minds to despair from the feelings we are experiencing. Whether it is anger, betrayal, despair, doubt, or pessimism, we allow these emotions to affect our hearts.

This should not happen to God's man "because the love of God has been poured out in our hearts." Whenever our hearts are troubled, we can rely upon God's love to see us through. This is why Jesus told His disciples on the night He was betrayed to not allow their hearts to be troubled.

God's man is a believer in Christ Jesus, and that means he can rely upon the omnipotence, omnipresence, and omniscience of God the Father.

If people know I am a Christian, and they should, then what does it tell them about my faith if I am prone to cultural despair? If I look at the depravity within American society and believe all is lost, how attractive is my faith to unbelievers?

It has become somewhat of a passing joke between many of my colleagues at work and me that when something in the news illustrates another example of cultural rot, they will say, "That person need Jesus, right Dave?"

That is because so often my response to many of us standing around "the water cooler," in this case the television in the break room discussing issues, where I'll say, "That person needs Jesus."

What I am trying to convey to people, mostly to myself, is that God is still on the throne and nothing takes Him by surprise. I want my responses to world events and my attitude at work to be one that testifies to the hope I have in Christ.

This is only possible by being clear-minded and steeped in biblical truth. It allows me to do as Peter has commanded:

"But sanctify the Lord God in your hearts, and always be ready to give a defense to everyone who asks you a reason for the hope that is in you, with meekness and fear." (1 Peter 3:15)

When my son Eddie was killed in Iraq, many people marveled at my family's and my faith. My response was that it wasn't our faith, but faith in a faithful God.

We knew because Eddie had given his life to Jesus Christ, that we would see him again in heaven. It is the blessed assurance that we have because we hope in Christ.

When people tell me they are sorry for losing my son, I tell them I haven't lost him; I know exactly where he is. He has just gone on before me. Some days I'm almost jealous of him.

Do you have that same blessed assurance? Does your family? If you were to die today, do you know where you'll spend eternity? Would your family be able to say they didn't lose you, but that you had gone onto heaven ahead of them?

If not, won't you receive that assurance right now by admitting that you have sinned, believing that Jesus Christ died for you, and confessing that Jesus Christ is Lord of your life?

Whether you're a new Christian or have been following Christ for a long time, has it manifested itself in your home becoming a heavenly refuge?

It's time to build a heavenly home...

Chapter Nine - Build Up!

"Unless the Lord builds the house, they labor in vain who build it."
(Psalm 127:1a)

An old Army buddy of mine had bought some property after he retired from active duty. The land was very usable, but the house itself was, let's just say, left a lot to be desired. He told me he was thinking of renovating it and asked my opinion (not that I'm well-versed in home renovations). My response was that I would move a mobile home in the backyard, bulldoze the whole house, and pray the foundation was still usable.

When we build our spiritual homes on a shaky foundation, life and/or Satan will come along and attempt to bulldoze it. Jesus warned us on the importance of a firm spiritual foundation:

"Therefore whoever hears these sayings of Mine, and does them, I will liken him to a wise man who built his house on the rock: and the rain descended, the floods came, and the winds blew and beat on that house; and it did not fall, for it was founded on the rock. But everyone who hears these sayings of Mine, and does not do them, will be like a foolish man who built his house on the sand: and the rain descended, the floods came, and the winds blew and beat on that house; and it fell. And great was its fall." (Matthew 7:24-27)

Satan and his minions on earth, both human and demonic, hate a godly home. Referring back to Steve Deace's book, *A Nefarious Plot*, as Demon General Nefarious, he writes:

> What I learned was the greatest strength and weakness of both the believer and unbeliever in your culture were the same—the family.

If you're having some doubt as to the validity of this, go back and read chapter 4, *Armor Up*, in this book. Satan wants to destroy all families, especially the Christian home.

This knowledge should put God's man on high alert. An alertness that manifests three required actions as the head of the household: edify, exemplify, and magnify.

Action #1: Edify

Idolatry is defined as worshiping anything other than the one true God. The examples of idols are endless, and as God's man and the spiritual leader of your home, it is your duty to find and remove them.

The Bible gives numerous examples of worshiping false gods and craven images. While this is still present in today's world among the lost masses, it is usually subtler when it comes to the Christian home. An idol always takes the place of God.

An idol can be materialistic, such as a car, boat, or even your home. It can be relational, such as with your children or wife. Your buddies can become an idol (more on that in the next chapter). One can even make an idol out of the Bible.

Regardless the form in which an idol has taken place in the home, God's man needs to find and remove it. However, just removing it is the first step. Something will eventually fill that void, so you must replace it with awe and reverence for God.

To do this, God must be edified, purposefully placed, as the most important person in your home:

"Give unto the Lord the glory due to His name; worship the Lord in the beauty of holiness." (Psalm 29:2)

Do you like wasting time? One of my biggest pet peeves is doing things I describe as "life drains." While some tasks may be menial, yet important to accomplish, there are many things we find ourselves doing that are complete wastes of time.

Trying to build your home without edifying God is the biggest waste of time. Go back and read again this chapter's verse. You cannot prominently place anything ahead of God and expect to have a godly home. Your labor is in vain.

Warning: the idols you discover and desire to remove may be, very likely will be, things your family cherishes. This will take love and patience on your part. You will need to sit your family down and explain what God is doing in your heart. Let them know that your greatest desire is to have a home that first and foremost edifies Almighty God.

Then you will be able to share with them the idols you have identified that must be removed. If you are prayed up before this meeting, asking God to give you His words and to prepare your family's hearts for the Truth, then you most likely will be surprised by their responses. Trust that the Lord will honor your efforts to build your home a holy one.

However, if you go off half-cocked like a tyrant demanding all "these evil idols" must go now, taking no prisoners, just because you've suddenly decided to follow God, expect the worse.

If you're not first displaying godliness in your home, you can't expect to immediately change things.

You have to show them the way.

Action #2: Exemplify

As a subject matter expert on leadership, I always teach young leaders they must set the example. You cannot expect a certain behavior if you do not demonstrate it. You must show the way.

Answering the question "Why" before it is even asked is always important. In the building of a solid, spiritual foundation of our home, show why it is important to exalt Jesus Christ above all.

The first reason you can give is because God the Father has exalted His Son:

"Therefore God also has highly exalted Him and given Him the name which is above every name." (Philippians 2:9)

God the Father has exalted the name of Jesus Christ above all other names. That could be the only reason we do so, but the Bible gives us more.

Getting caught up in the latest Christian trend happens to many Christian homes, be it music or some charismatic leader, but nothing and no one is greater than Jesus:

"I indeed baptize you with water unto repentance, but He who is coming after me is mightier than I, whose sandals I am not worthy to carry. He will baptize you with the Holy Spirit and fire."
(Matthew 3:11)

Remember that Jesus described John the Baptist as the greatest among men who was born of a woman. As God's man, I must personify the same humility of John the Baptist. I can never, as in ever, believe I am more important than Christ.

Now that may seem obvious, but obviously we are guilty of this at times. In my life, this manifests itself in my putting my opinion above Scripture. My opinion of Scripture is not important; I need to know what it says. As I always teach my Sunday school class, we don't get to determine the Bible's meaning; we are to discover it and then apply it to our lives.

Going back to discovering and removing idols in our home, it is important to teach our family that idolatry comes from a lack of contentment. Contentment with our God, our wife, our children, and our home will bring a satisfaction that is contagious to our family:

"Now godliness with contentment is great gain." (1 Timothy 6:6)

If God's man is constantly complaining about how broke down the house is, how badly the car needs to be replaced, or any other area of dissatisfaction, then it will spread like a germ.

However, if you are constantly thanking Jesus for your home, car, job, in general the blessed life you are living, that too will become infectious in a positive way.

Your family will see how fortunate they are to have a roof over their heads, an automobile that provides the necessary transportation for the family, and how God provides their every need. But it starts with *you* dear brothers.

To borrow a phrase from Chef Emeril Lagasse, it's time to kick it up a notch...

Action #3: Magnify

Are you familiar with the hymn *Count Your Blessings*? The refrain goes like this:

> *Count your blessings, name them one by one,*
> *Count your blessings, see what God has done!*
> *Count your blessing, name them one by one,*
> *Count your many blessing, see what God has done!*

I want you to take a moment to do that, right now. Get a piece of paper and fold it in half length-wise, just like you did in school. On the left side I want you to write and underline *Blessings.* On the right side I want you to write and underline *Curses.*

Now I want you to think of all the ways God has blessed you and any way that life has cursed you. In other words, what has brought calamity or tragedy, list those as curses. Go ahead and do this, take as much time as you need. I'll wait.

So what does your list look like? Are there more blessings than curses? This is an important starting point.

If you are going to deepen your appreciation for what God has done in your life, of course God's man should be focused on the spiritual aspect of his relationship with Jesus.

Notwithstanding, it is in our physical world, the practical way we live our lives, that we often get off track spiritually. When life gets hard, our worship can suffer. We tend to concentrate on those areas that challenge us the most. I have to have a way to keep my eyes on Jesus Christ and the life He provides me.

There is no greater way to magnify the Lord in your home when your family sees you going through a tough time. When they see that Dad isn't panicking over his and the family's circumstances, then they will have a quiet confidence.

I love the book and movie *A Christmas Carol* by Charles Dickens. One of my favorite scenes is when the Cratchit Family are gathered around the dinner table about to partake of Christmas dinner, and Bob Cratchit includes his tyrant of a boss Ebenezer Scrooge, in his prayer of thanksgiving. Mrs. Cratchit takes offense at the mention of Scrooge's name, but Bob will not have any of it.

Although dramatic as it may be of an example of gratitude, it's not too far off to where a godly man's heart should be. Even if we have a job and/or boss that is less than ideal, or even insufferable, if you are able to provide for your family you should portray a deep sense of gratitude for God's provision. James reminds us:

"Every good gift and every perfect gift is from above, and comes down from the Father of lights, with whom there is no variation or shadow of turning." (James 1:17)

If the only time our family sees us praising God is when things are going great, then their gratitude towards the Lord will be limited to only the good times. While we don't have to praise God for going through seasons of testing, we can thank Him for being there with us, leading the way. He holds the future in His hands!

On the other hand, if our wives and children see us "losing it" every time something goes wrong in life, we are going to spook them. This familial fear can manifest itself in a number of ways.

Your wife may keep bad news from you, a situation that requires your attention, for fear of your reaction. Your children may hide in their bedrooms if they know Dad is in a bad mood. The father always sets the temperature in the house. Dad is the spiritual thermostat that affects the rest of the family.

As long as God's man keeps his eyes on Jesus, his family will follow suit. The home will become a heavenly refuge instead of a hellish asylum.

All of the family will always look forward to going home.

Additionally, your most important human relationship will deepen and grow exponentially.

Your wife will truly become your best friend and confidant.

Let the romance begin!

Chapter Ten - Make Up!

"Husbands, likewise, dwell with them with understanding, giving honor to the wife, as to the weaker vessel, and as being heirs together of the grace of life, that your prayers may not be hindered."
(1 Peter 3:7)

If he is married, the most important human being in the life of God's man is his bride. While it is true our wives can sometimes be a mystery to solve, which makes a marriage interesting, the Bible gives many clues on a husband's duties.

Contrary to some postmodern theological teachings, God designed marriage. After He created Adam and saw man alone in the garden, God then gave Adam a wife:

"And the Lord God said, 'It is not good that man should be alone; I will make him a helper comparable to him.'" (Genesis 2:18)

The Hebrew word for helper is *ezer* and literally translated means *help meet* or *one who helps*. A better word to describe the helper would be *partner*. This is why a few verses later we read God's ordination of marriage:

"Therefore a man shall leave his father and mother and be joined to his wife, and they shall become one flesh." (Genesis 2:24)

The Hebrew word for *joined* not only means what we understand the word to mean in Modern English, but it also means to "pursue closely; to overtake; to catch." The King James Version renders it as *cleave.*

Cleaving to our wives is a lifetime commitment and challenge. A marriage that has gone stale is one where God's man has stop pursuing his bride. He has forgotten the charge Peter has given the husband in our verse at the top of the page.

To give honor to our wife means to consider her as precious and valuable. We should show and shower our bride with this honor. We give reverence to her as the gift from God she is.

If not, then not only does our home life suffer, but also our prayer life will suffer.

Perhaps you are completely confused how to love your wife as Christ loved the church as we are commanded in Ephesians 5:25. Obviously, many a book has been written on this subject, but for the purposes of this chapter and brevity, I've narrowed the subject down to three areas the Bible addresses.

If God's man's will either begin or improve in these three areas, then he will see a strengthening in his marriage. Husbands must make their wives feel safe, secure, and special.

Area #1: Safe

What did the Apostle Peter mean when he described the wife as "the weaker vessel?" It literally means the woman is physically weaker than the man. It does not mean the husband is spiritually or morally superior to the wife. Sadly, that is often not the case. There may be a few exceptions to the husband's physical prowess over his wife, but generally speaking the man is physically stronger than the woman.

This means God's man must protect his wife like the princess she is. She is a precious gift from God, a beautiful, fragile, invaluable vessel that should be treated as such.

A wife should feel the safest when she is home. Regardless the type of home, husbands are to provide a home where the wife feels protected. God's man must provide a home that is safe.

If God's man is following Christ's lead, he will receive the Lord's direction on how to be a good husband to his wife.

When I learn how much the Lord Jesus Christ loves me as His church, which is the bride of Christ, it inspires me to love my wife as such. I receive not only the inspiration to do so, but also the qualification. We can aspire to be great husbands, but we must be molded by the Holy Spirit to actually perform as such.

As the head of the household, the husband must take charge of the home and the children. This is how we earn the respect of our wives; something husbands greatly desire and need.

Your family may not always appreciate your rules, but rules are what make for a safe home environment. I have told many a husband if you have to eat dinner on the back patio because everyone is mad at you, so be it. Stand your ground!

Your rules are not to subdue your family and suck the joy out of the home; it is to set up protective boundaries. This is true even without children. The earlier you establish yourself as the head of the household, the more natural it will be to defer to Dad when children do arrive.

Being the protector of the home does not mean being some macho man, looking for trouble wherever he can stir it up. God's man displays Christian courage in a Christlike manner. Of course, every husband and father should protect the physical lives of his family, but he must also spiritually protect them.

A safe home is one that is protected from the principalities, powers, and rulers of darkness in the present age. That means what our family listens to, reads, and watches must be spiritually edifying.

Any entertainment that uses profanity, pornography, or depravity must be purged from the home. Always use Paul's measure to decide if something is suitable for your home:

"Finally, brethren, whatever things are true, whatever things are noble, whatever things are just, whatever things are pure, whatever things are lovely, whatever things are of good report, if there is any virtue and if there is anything praiseworthy—meditate on these things."
(Philippians 4:8)

Depending on your wife's spiritual maturity, she may resist such "censoring." You will have to lovingly explain the protection and provision behind your rules. Help her to understand that it is for her spiritual well-being. Eventually, your wife will not only come to understand you are concerned for her safety, but she will also experience a new sense of emotional security.

Action #2: Secure

The greatest emotional security God's man can give to his bride is to make her feel loved. While saying you love your wife is always important, the adage actions speaks louder than words was never truer than when it comes to how you treat your wife.

While financial security is important, what our brides need more than a stable home budget is emotional and relational security. Too often God's man is so focused on financially providing for his family he ends up neglecting his wife's emotional needs, thus hurting his marital relationship. If you need clarification on your duties as provider, go back and read Chapter 1 again.

To make your wife feel emotionally secure, she must know that she is number one in your life, second only to Jesus Christ. That means "going out with the boys" on a regular basis has to stop.

The occasional Christian men's outing is fine; I'm talking about meeting up with the fellas on a regular basis. If you think this keeps the flame lit in your marriage (I've actually been told that), then you need a new lighter. Your buddies should never have higher or equal priority with your wife.

If you're feeling resistance to what I'm telling you, answer me this: what human relationship is the most important in your life? If you said your wife, but still think you should be able to go out with the boys on a regular basis, then your words are speaking louder than your actions.

Dear brother, your buddies should be at best number five on your list of relational priorities. Here's a list to help you clear up any stinking thinking you may have about relationships:

1. Jesus Christ
2. Wife
3. Children
4. Relatives
5. Friends

When your bride realizes that you love Jesus first and then her, she'll not only know she has a godly man for a husband, she'll also feel secure in her marriage. Why? This action brings heavenly joy to the home:

"Live joyfully with the wife whom you love all the days of your vain life which He has given you under the sun, all your days of vanity; for that is your portion in life, and in the labor which you perform under the sun." (Ecclesiastes 9:9)

King Solomon is teaching marriage is a lifetime commitment. Even though life can be difficult and is short, but a breath (the meaning of *vanity*), it can be a joy. A home where the husband and wife love each other is one filled with great joy.

Solomon is trying to teach us not to make the same mistakes he did. Writing Ecclesiastes, he is coming to the end of his life and looking at all the wasted time he spent chasing temporal pleasures and riches. Solomon had over 1,000 wives and concubines, but he knew better. Solomon understood God's design for marriage; he wrote the book Song of Solomon.

Knowing better and doing better are two different things. Solomon disobeyed God's teachings and got his priorities cross-threaded. At the end of his life he is reminding God's man that marriage should be placed only after his relationship with God.

Dear brother, there is no greater way to provide emotional security to your wife than to prove to her every day, or at least strive to, that she is the most important human in your life.

I promise you if you will do this, you'll be making her feel special.

Action #3: Special

May I ask you a personal question? When was the last time your wife and you went out on a date? You may be thinking, well we go to dinner and a movie. Okay, that's a good start. Next time, make it a date, and not just on the occasion of a birthday or anniversary (although you never want to miss those!).

I'm talking taking your bride to a nice restaurant (it doesn't have to be expensive), to a movie of her choice (remember, you're trying to make her feel special), and then going for a walk afterwards, holding hands and delighting in her company.

You do remember doing that, right? Hopefully that is how you courted her before she said yes to your marriage proposal. How often do you think your bride remembers those times? Does she watch Hallmark movies? If yes, it's because those romance movies remind her of you! I'm literally realizing this as I write it.

My courtship with Karen was precious. We so delighted in each other; I literally adored her. I still do, and I praise God that my adoration for her is stronger than when we dated. However, my overt actions to show that adoration have not always been a priority for me. I want to change that. I hope you do as well with your bride. Reminisce dear brother of your courtship with her.

If she asks why this sudden change in you, tell her exactly why. Tell her that you missed courting her and that you want to rekindle that in your relationship. Talk about keeping the flame lit; brother, your lighter just turned into a flamethrower!

If you think for a minute your bride doesn't look like she did when you were courting her, take a quick look in the mirror. We good now? Your bride has grown an inner beauty that should be apparent to you, if you will only look:

"You have ravished my heart, my sister, my spouse; you have ravished my heart with one look of your eyes, with one link of your necklace."
(Song of Solomon 4:9)

Go back and read Song of Solomon 4:1-15; that's some pretty "racy" love language Solomon is using. You might not want to tell your bride that her "hair is like a flock of goats," but you can complement her on how pretty she looks. Oh, and be sure not to say, "You look pretty today dear." The reason should be obvious.

Most Christian men know they are to love their wives as Christ loved the church, but do they know why? Too often we stop at verse 25 in Ephesians 5, which is the command. The important reason for the command follows in the succeeding five verses:

"Husbands, love your wives, just as Christ also loved the church and gave Himself for her, that He might sanctify and cleanse her with the washing of water by the word, that He might present her to Himself a glorious church, not having spot or wrinkle or any such thing, but that she should be holy and without blemish. So husbands ought to love their own wives as their own bodies; he who loves his wife loves himself. For no one ever hated his own flesh, but nourishes and cherishes it, just as the Lord does the church."
(Ephesians 5:25-30)

Letting our wives know that we still find them attractive is important. However, of the utmost importance is our bride's spiritual well-being. This is what Paul alludes to in our passage.

Paul is reminding God's man that Jesus gave His life sacrificially for us the Church, known as His Bride. If I will follow Jesus' model of loving my wife, I will give myself to her. It means I will sacrificially love her, doing whatever it takes to make her feel safe, secure, and special. But there's more...

Paul continues in verse 26 and says I am to "sanctify" my wife by cleansing "her with the washing of water by the word." God's man is the spiritual leader and he should use the Word of God to establish the household. The Word of God sets us apart as we constantly grow in its Truth.

Husband and wife are imperfect people. It all began in the Garden of Eden, when Eve did not rightly divide God's Word when the serpent misquoted it. In fact, Eve not only did not correct Satan when he misquoted Scripture, she added to it.

This is what Paul meant when he wrote of the church "not having spot or wrinkle or any such thing." The only way to iron out erroneous teaching and thinking is through "the washing of water by the word." This happens through the Spirit of God using the Word of God.

Dear brothers, this is how we find satisfaction in our marriages. Whatever we do to our brides, we do to ourselves. That is what it means to love our wives as our own bodies. If what we do is loving and nurturing, we satisfy each other. The opposite brings only disappointment and failure in our duties as husband.

If you have yet to been blessed with children, now is a perfect time to strengthen your relationship with your wife. If children are already part of your family, then you have some catching up to do. You can't make up for lost time, but you can get to where God desires you to be, not only as a husband, but also as a father.

Time to train up our children...

Chapter Eleven - Train Up!

"Train up a child in the way he should go, and when he is old he will not depart from it." (Proverbs 22:6)

When my children were younger, we used to play a little game called, "That's a no." Whenever we would go to the mall, our shopping trip would always end at the food court having either lunch or at least a snack. One day, I saw some teenagers who clearly were not living in a Proverbs 22:6 home.

I pointed towards that group and said, "See those teenagers over there? That's a no." I was telling my children I would not allow that type of behavior in our home. After that, during subsequent mall visits, *they* would point out and say, "That's a no, right Dad."

This little game was not meant to belittle those other children. My heart did and still does break for children who grow up in a home without the loving discipline and guidance of a godly father. Trust me, I know what it's like to live that life. I almost waited too long to be that type of father with my own children.

Too many parents want to be their children's friends. Let me give each of you godly fathers (and mothers eavesdropping on this) some advice.

They already have friends. They need you to be a parent. When they become adults they will become your friends.

How does that happen? If your children are living under your roof, you sit in the seat of authority. When they leave, you sit in the seat of counsel. See the difference?

One is your responsibility as their parent; the other is your privilege as a parent. Rarely is it joyful to discipline your children. Rarely is it not joyful to counsel them as adults.

"Whoever loves wisdom makes his father rejoice, but a companion of harlots wastes his wealth." (Proverbs 29:3)

How do you keep your children from going astray? How do you teach them the biblical precepts and principles that will bring protection and provision to their lives? While there are no guarantees in life, the Bible addresses three responsibilities of a father. When it comes to raising children, fathers must domesticate, educate, and liberate.

Responsibility #1: Domesticate

There are at least three verses in the Book of Proverbs that talks of "sparing the rod." Proverbs 23:13 even uses the words, "If you beat him with a rod, he will not die."

Let me clear up the obvious: this does not give the father the authority to beat his child. Discipline is not physical abuse.

Discipline *does* include spankings.

So what is the "rod?" It is something that won't harm your child, such as a paddle. I used a paddle ball paddle, you remember those. The paddle had a ball hooked to a rubber band that you could get the ball bouncing really fast off the paddle.

The late, great lion of faith Dr. Adrian Rogers suggested using something other than your hand so that your child will always connect your hand with a loving touch and the actual "rod" with the discipline.

Discipline is meant to correct bad behavior and reinforce the necessity of good behavior. I know you see your toddler as a little angel, but you didn't have to teach him or her how to say "no." You don't have to teach your children how to be bad; they got that down pat. As the old Buck Owens' country and western song says, "All I have to do is act naturally."

Hard as it may believe the day your child is born, they come into this world with a sin nature. It's hereditary. Without loving, biblical correction, children will grow up lacking discipline:

"Chasten your son while there is hope, and do not set your heart on his destruction." (Proverbs 19:18)

A godly father who takes his time to teach his children not only biblical precepts and principles, but also the biblical protection and provision from obeying God, will reap great joy later in life. His children will honor him when they get older. They will seek his advice in important matters of adulthood.

Before we go to the next section, take time to read Deuteronomy 6. It is a short chapter, but very important in understanding our role as godly fathers. Additionally, I recommend you buy Josh McDowell and Bob Hostettler's book, "Right from Wrong." Both will become valuable resources for you to refer to often.

Responsibility #2: Educate

Another lesson I taught my children was in the decision-making area. Whenever they were presented with what could seem an ethical dilemma, I gave them this simple rule: "If it takes more than 30 seconds to justify an action, it's probably wrong."

I knew this to be good advice because in my own life I had both heeded and ignored it. Guess which time worked out best for me? Yes, ignoring your conscience, particularly if you're a born-again Christian, is not the path to righteousness:

"A wise son heeds his father's instruction, but a scoffer does not listen to rebuke." (Proverbs 13:1)

Teaching our children how to live righteous lives is not just correcting bad behavior; it is also encouraging good behavior. A godly father's love can never be conditional. Let me explain.

When my son Eddie was around 15 years old, he was living with his mother in Alabama. I was stationed in Germany with my wife Karen.

I forget what the certain behavior was, but I harshly scolded Eddie in an email. His response crushed me: "I'm sorry I'm not the son you wanted me to be." This was not some lame attempt to make me feel sorry for him. Somehow his brokenness came across to me in his words. I sat at my desk and wept.

I cried out to God: "Father, I'm blowing this with my son. How do I fix this?!" Through the Holy Spirit, God gently answered: "Love him like I love you; unconditionally."

I immediately emailed my son back and asked him to forgive me. I told him that my love for him will never be based on his performance. I would always love and treasure him as a gift from God.

My son's knowing that I would always love him changed our relationship forever. Later, Eddie told me that because of my unconditional love, he wanted to strive to be a better man.

He wanted to be like me. I'm weeping now as I fondly remember how God taught me how to love my son. Little did I know that day we would have only 8 short years left together on earth. Nevertheless, our bond grew so strong, that Eddie eventually became my best, male friend. Until he went to be with Jesus, we grew as brothers-in-Christ.

What I didn't realize with my harsh email, was that I had done to Eddie what Paul admonished fathers against doing:

"And you, fathers, do not provoke your children to wrath, but bring them up in the training and admonition of the Lord." (Ephesians 6:4)

Notice Paul didn't say to "bring them up in the training and the admonition of Dave." I tried that and it totally backfired on me and hurt my son.

However, when I reached out to the Lord and sought His counsel, He not only taught me how to biblically train and admonish my children, more importantly His instruction provided heavenly salve for my son and me.

The greatest struggle for most godly men is not in the biblical training of our children; there are many great resources available for teaching our children godly character. If this isn't happening in a Christian home it is usually lack of desire and not lack of ability. That can and should be quickly overcome.

How to admonish our children is where the great challenge always presented itself to me. I know that Ephesians 6:4 and Colossians 3:21 warn me to not provoke my children to the point of discouragement, but how do I admonish them?

The Greek word for admonition is *nouthesia*, and it denotes a "mild rebuke or warning." It means we call attention to a certain unacceptable behavior without berating our child. When we admonish our children, it should be a teachable moment.

Notice I didn't say an opportunity to lecture.

We must teach our children why it is important to behave a certain way, how God's instruction protects us from dangerous behavior and provides us a way to righteous living.

Training and admonition bring us to the ultimate goal in Proverbs 22:6; when our children grow old, they will not depart from biblical instruction.

Eventually, your child will become an adult and you are going to have to set him or her free into the world. You can do so confidently knowing you've raised a Proverbs 22:6 child.

Responsibility #3: Liberate

There are days when I reminisce about my children when they were little. I have sweet memories of Eddie and Becky as wee little ones, cackling with laughter over something silly their daddy did. I look at my stepdaughter (I call her my bonus daughter) Tiffany and marvel how far she's come from the shy thirteen year old I first met. Watching all three of them get together and have fun always brought such great joy to Karen and me, especially their comedy routines.

Nevertheless, my three adult children have easily brought me more joy as I've watched them grow up. Although Eddie went to heaven much too soon, I still have fond memories of the man he became. My two girls are amazing and beautiful women, both very successful in their professions.

Karen and I had to learn in a hurry that once they went off to college, we had to start letting go of our authority over them. We had to trust that the life lessons we strived to teach them would serve them well. We had to come to understand that they would have their successes and failures and the best we could do is share them and not protect them.

My prayer for my children before they graduated high school was they would find God's path for their lives and that the Lord would give them godly spouses. My continual prayer is that their lives would end as King Jehoshaphat's did:

"And he walked in the way of his father Asa, and did not turn aside from it, doing what was right in the sight of the Lord."
(2 Chronicles 20:32)

Man of God, as a father your most important job is to teach your children the value of following the Lord Jesus Christ. You cannot command them to do so; you have to show them the way.

It should be a normal sight for your children to see you reading your Bible, to hear you openly praise and pray to the Lord, and to stand on the truth of His Word. In other words, you have to model the life you want them to live. This includes humility, integrity, and nobility.

That means I don't wear my badge of humility proudly. It means admitting when I'm wrong and seeking forgiveness from those I wrong, especially my children.

Integrity is displayed before my children when I'm the same person at home that I am at church. It means not being a hypocrite.

Nobility means I am a man of superior character, not as compared to others. My standards are what God sets for me in His Word. I should be the godliest man my children know.

If I have strived to be God's man before my children, I can release my children out into the world like the arrows they are described as in Psalms:

"Like arrows in the hand of a warrior, so are the children of one's youth. Happy is the man who has his quiver full of them; they shall not be ashamed, but shall speak with their enemies in the gate."
(Psalm 127:4-5)

I can almost feel the anxiety and tension of those reading this, especially the mothers. Please understand that when your children leave your house into adulthood, your seat of authority leaves with them. If there is tension between your adult child and you, it might be because you are trying to sit in a "chair" that no longer exists.

However, if you've raised a Proverbs 22:6 child there will be a much more comfortable and satisfying "chair" in which to sit. The seat of counsel is a parent's reward for raising godly children. A Proverbs 31 woman is called blessed by her children.

God's man should have a heart like Solomon's towards his children:

"My son, if your heart is wise, my heart will rejoice—indeed, I myself; yes, my inmost being will rejoice when your lips speak right things."
(Proverbs 23:15-16)

Perhaps you missed your chance to be that father with your children. If they have already left your home, it's not too late to influence their lives. They still need a godly father, one whom they can turn to when they need advice. They need to know they will receive understanding when they mess up, and solid biblical counsel on how to get back on the path of righteousness.

This is a tall order. All eleven chapters are a challenge. They were a challenge to write, to ensure that I didn't come across as holier than thou, but transparent, sharing my struggles and the lessons God taught me.

I came to a point in my life where God wanted to know if I was ready to become His man. I hope and pray you find yourself at that point now. If so, then it's time to go on to the last chapter.

If not, and this is no small request I am making, I recommend you start this book over. At the very least, go back to the table of contents and determine what areas you still need to work on.

However, if your heart is set on being God's man, even if you have reservations about your abilities, then please continue. God doesn't need your abilities; He needs your availability.

The Lord is looking for godly men; will He find you?

Chapter Twelve - Show Up!

"Run to and fro through the streets of Jerusalem; see now and know;
and seek in her open places if you can find a man, if there
is anyone who executes judgment, who seeks the truth,
and I will pardon her." (Jeremiah 5:1)

As I write this it is Independence Day, 2018. Thinking of our nation ridding itself of the despotic bondage of England, I am reminded of an encounter I had last Friday.

I was returning from Pensacola after having lunch with two dear brothers-in-Christ. On my way, I stopped at a convenience store to buy a cup of coffee. A man who looked familiar to me, somewhat disheveled and sweaty, approach me with a smile.

He asked me what I was buying and I told some iced coffee, and I asked him if we knew each other. He asked me where I had been in the world, and I told him I had been many places in the Army.

Then I remembered where I knew him from; we used to attend a Saturday morning men's prayer breakfast at a local air force base chapel. He remembered that and asked if we could speak after my purchase.

He was sitting over in the restaurant area of the store waiting on a chicken dinner order. I asked what he'd been up to, and he told me he'd just got off work repairing boats.

He told me his 81-year old mother was in the hospital battling pancreatic cancer. He had just finished a beer and had another one in a brown paper bag. He said a kind gentleman had bought them for him.

He had fallen on hard times. Hard times of his own making. He didn't admit to this last sentence; I would remind him of that in a few minutes.

He was trying to get to the hospital to see his mother, but needed to get home, shower up, and then find a way to the hospital.

I bought his lunch for him, and offered him a ride home or to the hospital, whichever he wanted. He asked to go home.

On the way, we chatted about his mother. I told him I would pray for her; my oldest sister had succumbed to pancreatic cancer.

I felt compelled to give him twenty dollars to get a cab to see his mother. I had no idea if he would use the money for that or to go buy a 12-pack of beer. I told him as much.

I told him what I did know is that he *knew* better than to be drinking beer and not attending church regularly, of which he earlier confessed he had not.

I told him, whether or not he actually knew the Lord Jesus Christ as his personal savior, he knew the way to Him.

I told him I knew this because I had seen him multiple times sitting under the teaching of the Word. I told him as a man of God he should not be in the situation he currently finds himself.

We shook hands, he thanked me, and I encouraged him to find his way back to Jesus.

I share this encounter because this man has left the scene. What scene you ask? The one where God is looking for His men to show up.

The Lord is looking for godly men; will He find you?

It's not as though the Lord has lost track of you. Every morning God has a roll call for godly men, where they receive their daily marching orders to plant the banner of Christ wherever they may be headed that particular day.

He is looking for godly men to courageously stand up in the faith.

He is looking for godly men to awaken and face the spiritual warfare of this present darkness.

He is looking for godly men to begin each day speaking with Him.

He is looking for godly men to armor up and prepare for the day.

He is looking for godly men to be students of the Bible.
He is looking for godly men to grow in fellowship with the Lord Jesus Christ.

He is looking for godly men to approach His throne from our prayer rooms.

He is looking for godly men to clear up the stinking thinking with the Truth of Jesus Christ.

He is looking for godly men to build our homes on a biblical foundation.

He is looking for godly men to love their wives as Christ loves the Church.

He is looking for godly men to teach our children the ways of the Lord.

Brother, God is looking for you to show up!

Yes, I just reviewed the previous chapters of this book and you may be looking at this list wondering where to begin.

Let me give you three areas in which to start: study, steady, simplify.

Area #1: Study

I would encourage you to go back and read Chapter 3 *Rise Up* again. After you do that, I want you to fill out the short covenant below to commit to staring each day in Scripture.

I'm going to give you a very simple Bible study to begin with after you sign the covenant:

I, _____, commit to Jesus Christ, to start each morning reading my Bible for at least 15 minutes for no less than a month. I make this commitment with the full expectation that the Holy Spirit will increase my appetite for God's Word and grow in my desire and love for Scripture.

Signed_____Date:_____

So here's the plan. On the next page is your daily Bible reading plan. Whatever day it is, that is the date I want you to begin at:

1st – Proverbs 1 and Psalms 1-5
2nd – Proverbs 2 and Psalms 6-10
3rd – Proverbs 3 and Psalms 11-15
4th – Proverbs 4 and Psalms 16-20
5th – Proverbs 5 and Psalms 21-25
6th – Proverbs 6 and Psalms 26-30
7th – Proverbs 7 and Psalms 31-35
8th – Proverbs 8 and Psalms 36-40
9th – Proverbs 9 and Psalms 41-45
10th – Proverbs 10 and Psalms 46-50
11th – Proverbs 11 and Psalms 51-55
12th – Proverbs 12 and Psalms 56-60
13th – Proverbs 13 and Psalms 61-65
14th – Proverbs 14 and Psalms 66-70
15th – Proverbs 15 and Psalms 71-75
16th – Proverbs 16 and Psalms 76-80
17th – Proverbs 17 and Psalms 81-85
18th – Proverbs 18 and Psalms 86-90
19th – Proverbs 19 and Psalms 91-95
20th – Proverbs 20 and Psalms 96-100
21st – Proverbs 21 and Psalms 101-105
22nd – Proverbs 22 and Psalms 106-110
23rd – Proverbs 23 and Psalms 111-115
24th – Proverbs 24 and Psalms 116-120 (skip Psalm 119)
25th – Proverbs 25 and Psalms 121-125
26th – Proverbs 26 and Psalms 126-130
27th – Proverbs 27 and Psalms 131-135
28th – Proverbs 28 and Psalms 136-140
29th – Proverbs 29 and Psalms 141-145
30th – Proverbs 30 and Psalms 146-150
31st – Proverbs 31 and Psalm 119 *

* In the months of February, April, June, September, and November you can make up the lost days on a Sunday.

I've listed this somewhat obvious plan because I want you to check off each day as you go. Don't read and check off each day as a way to meet your commitment. Do it so you can see the progress you are making. Nothing helps us to reach our goals quicker than to track our progress.

Our goal is to become a student of the Scriptures, to develop a hunger and love for God's Word. We are children of the Most High God, and we should claim our full inheritance:

"Therefore, laying aside all malice, all deceit, hypocrisy, envy, and all evil speaking, as newborn babes, desire the pure milk of the word, that you may grow thereby, if indeed you have tasted that the Lord is gracious." (1 Peter 2:1-3)

Why does Peter advise us to lay down the obvious sins he's listed in the above passage? Christians who are acting in this manner are nothing more the pretenders.

Peter is talking about deceitful men, attempting to manipulate others to satiate their evil desires. God's Word will not only remove such ungodly qualities, but it will bring a steadiness to our lives.

Area #2: Steady

If he hasn't already started planting excuses in your mind, Satan will surely try to trip you up as you make your way to God's Daily Roll Call.

In fact, if the devil isn't already giving you reason to doubt your ability to make this sojourn, it's because you are not seriously considering it. Let's get that straight before we continue on. Go back and read the covenant you signed. Is that your name on the line? Did you date it? Okay, any questions?

Now that your commitment and resolve are strong, how do you avoid Satan's pitfalls and traps? Solomon provides the answer:

"Let your eyes look straight ahead, and your eyelids look right before you. Ponder the path of your feet, and let all your ways be established. Do not turn to the right or the left; remove your foot from evil."

(Proverbs 4:25-27)

When doubt and indecision creep their way into your life, the first place your walk with Christ will suffer will be in your quiet and study time. Other idols will replace this covenantal time you have carved out for yourself. Jesus warns us:

"No one, having put his hand to the plow, and looking back, is fit for the kingdom of God." (Luke 9:62)

A steadfast heart is needed if we are going to be present every day at God's Roll Call. How do I make sure that I become this disciplined in my daily studies and walk with Jesus?

I harken back to my Basic Combat Training when I first came into the Army. When I arrived to Fort Knox, Kentucky and received my military uniforms and boots, they took away all my personal belongings, minus my watch and wallet. They allowed nothing from the outside world to interfere with my basic training. All distractions were removed.

In other words, they simplified my life so I could concentrate on becoming a soldier. If we are going to become good soldiers for Jesus, then we may need to take a less radical approach, but a similar approach nevertheless. We need to simplify our lives.

Area #3: Simplify

What keeps you from getting up fifteen minutes early each morning to get into God's Word? I would imagine it is television, or perhaps a video game, or some other technological gadget that keeps you up past your bedtime.

I recommend you get yourself 7 to 8 hours of sleep each day. Too hard for you to pull off?

If you're burning that candle from both ends, brother eventually the flames are going to meet and something is going to get burned. In this case, it will be your morning time with the Lord.

No matter the cause for the burn, it is unbearable and unnecessary. Nothing, as in no one thing, is worth jeopardizing your growth as God's man. You need to discover the distraction and remove it.

As I wrote in Chapter 9 *Build Up*, this doesn't mean you have to go on a rampage and throw the TV, X-Box, and iPad into the garbage. You are capable of controlling yourself without such harsh measures. You just have to purpose in your heart to do so.

I love baseball. No, I *love* baseball. I am an avid San Francisco Giants fan. I have the MLB Premium channel, to which I can watch every Giants game on any device, broadcast from my hometown network. There's one problem though. Most of their games don't come on until 9:35 pm my time.

That means if I'm going to get at least 7 hours of sleep, I need to turn out the lights by 10 pm. That means at best I can get 2 innings in before I need to go to sleep.

Too often the game draws me in and I want to stay up and watch. Most times I just don't turn it on. Other times, I'm able to shut it off and turn out the lights.

Either way, I have to make the decision that my sleep is vital because the most important thing in my life is waiting for me in the morning; my quiet and study time with the Lord.

Why do I consider this the most important thing in my life? This time with the Lord is part of the inheritance of being adopted into God's family.

How foolish would it be to not receive all that is rightfully mine as a child of God?

"And whatever you do, do it heartily, as to the Lord and not to men, knowing that from the Lord you will receive the reward of the inheritance; for you serve the Lord Christ." (Colossians 3:23-24)

We've been on a journey, one that I pray has brought you to a place of resolution and recommitment. If I have done my job as I proposed in the introduction, then the following has happened:

1. The Holy Spirit has illuminated your heart and mind and given you a new desire to be God's man.

2. Your passion for the Lord Jesus Christ as been reignited.

3. The fire in your belly to be in God's Word daily has been rekindled.

4. You have already begun seeking the answers to life's daily questions.

Go back and read Jeremiah 5:1 at the beginning of this chapter. As you read Jeremiah 5 in its totality, you discover the Prophet Jeremiah has been sent by God on an investigatory mission. He was to search "the streets of Jerusalem" to see if he could find any men who rightly judges and "seeks the truth."

Jeremiah's mission was a complete failure. He was unable to find one, not *one* man, who was honest and truthful.

So what's the application to us today? I believe it is simple.

The Lord Jesus Christ is looking for godly men.

Will He find you?

Afterword

"Man Up! What the Bible Says About Being A Man" shouts to the reader, "Don't quit, you can achieve full manhood to the glory of God!

The author establishes the foundational truth that one may be born male but only the Spirit of God through the Word of God can reveal God's plan for manhood.

Thus, manhood is a quest. This work, while addressing the joy of beginning the quest for manhood, wisely focuses on the middle mile which tests and molds a man's character.

Through his own personal journey and sound Biblical application, the author presents a compelling case that it is through the dreary middle mile of life that godly manhood is achieved or lost.

Thus each chapter carries the reader onward, providing practical steps, a biblical roadmap of God's design to stay the course.

With unwavering conviction, David encourages the reader to claim Jesus Christ as his model for manhood, rely upon His strength and refuse to limp through life.

The call is clear...Man Up!

Dr. Dennis Brunet
Senior Pastor
Midway Baptist Church
Gulf Breeze, Florida

About the Author

Amazon best-selling author Dave Jeffers is a Sunday School Teacher, Bible student, and lay preacher. Dave graduated magna cum laude from Liberty University with a bachelor's degree in religion. Dave received cum laude honors at Liberty Baptist Theological Seminary with a M.A. in Theological Studies.

Dave has written a year-long series of 30 day devotionals titled *Eavesdropping on God: One Man's Conversations with the Lord.* All twelve books, as well as other works, are available on Amazon. Please visit Dave's Amazon author page for more information.

To book Dave for speaking engagements, please email him at:
jeffers221@bellsouth.net

YOU ARE INVITED TO EAVESDROP ON ONE MAN'S LIFE, AND EVEN THOUGH THESE ARE HIS CONVERSATIONS WITH GOD, YOU WILL BE AMAZED AND BLESSED BY THEIR APPLICATION TO YOUR EVERYDAY LIFE.

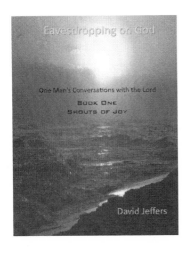

Book One: Shouts of Joy
Covers moments of joy experienced by the author...

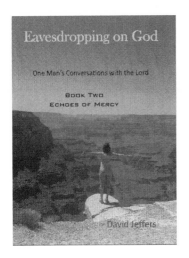

Book Two:
Echoes of Mercy
Covers how God's mercy covered the author's life and blessed him beyond measure...

Book Three:
Whispers of Grace
*Covers how God's grace
redeemed the author's life,
bringing God's abundant
blessings…*

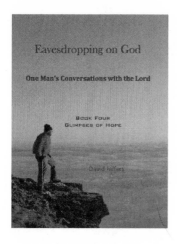

Book Four:
Glimpses of Hope
*Covers how hope in God
sustains the author's life,
giving him the blessed hope
that is in Christ…*

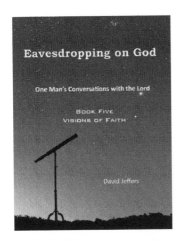

Book Five:
Visions of Faith
Teaches how the unseen can become evident in our walk with Christ, thus growing our faith in the Lord...

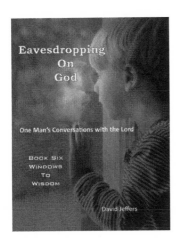

Book Six:
Windows to Wisdom
Shares Biblical treasures of wisdom nuggets...

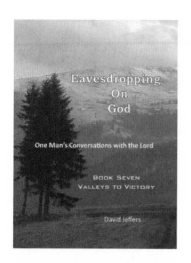

Book Seven:
Valleys to Victory
Most Christians desire only mountaintop experiences with God, but life isn't all mountaintops...

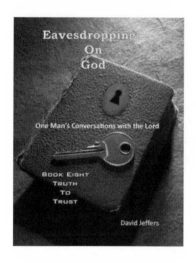

Book Eight:
Truth to Trust
Absolute truth, of which Jesus spoke, has always been, is, and always will be alive and real...

Book Nine:
Feelings of Forgiveness
We cannot experience forgiveness if we refuse to forgive…

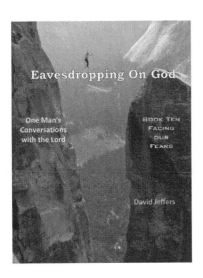

Book Ten:
Facing Our Fears
Misplaced fears can cause us to abandon God's ways and seek our own answers…

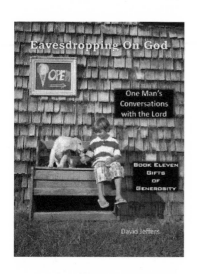

Book Eleven:
Gifts of Generosity
Imagine when you get to heaven that Jesus says you were generous to a fault...

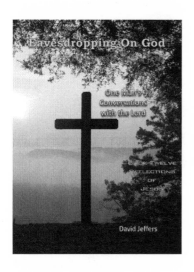

Book Twelve:
Reflections of Jesus
How do we become Christlike? We must know and love Him. We have to be of one mind with Jesus...

Made in the USA
Columbia, SC
02 December 2018